A PACIFIC LOVE

SERAG MONIER

This is the English translation of the Arabic novel عشق في جنوب الهادي originally published in Egypt in 2021 by Elbasheer publishing darelbasheer.net

First edition March 2022
Translated by Eman Thabet
Edited by: Brooks Becker, Omar Ibrahim
Cover art by: 100covers.com
Layout by: Charlyn Samson

Contents

ARWA—CAIRO, FEBRUARY 2017

Tuesday mornings are the worst part of the week! I struggle to get up while vowing to quit my job, stay at home, and wait for my potential future husband to show up. The building's elevator is always tiny and suffocating. On Tuesdays, it feels even tinier, as if it goes through some weekly cycle, where it gradually shrinks throughout the week until it reaches the peak of its narrowness on Tuesdays, then it goes back to expanding once again.

My car is also noisier than usual on that day, and the drivers around me are at their most reckless state of mind as if they're all competing in some Formula auto race. On this Tuesday, one driver looked in my direction as we were both stuck in traffic before he shoved an obnoxious smile down my throat. Yes, I mean it when I say he "shoved" his smile; that's exactly how it felt when that unpleasant smile appeared on his face, then shot in my direction to ram violently into my face. I shut the window, turned off the radio, put on a song by Mayada

Al-Hennawy[1], and tried to focus on enjoying it until I reached the headquarters of the company.

The company's elevator goes through a similar shrinking weekly cycle, but it's even more crowded than the one in my building. On Tuesdays, it reaches the peak of both its tininess and capacity, but since I was more than half an hour late, there was no one in the elevator except me and him. I wasn't able to examine his facial features thoroughly, since it wasn't appropriate to stare with just the two of us in the elevator. I did, however, assume that he might be in his late forties, as I noticed those grey hairs covering both sides of his head. He had subtle crow's feet at the corners of his eyes and some fine lines between his eyebrows. His thin-framed glasses, which rested on a slightly plump nose and a round face, concealed some of those lines.

The elevator traveled slowly, as I felt some sort of awkwardness regarding the two of us being alone together, which was an unexpected feeling I was experiencing for the first time. He was a well-mannered gentleman who avoided staring and didn't attempt to initiate a conversation. I did, however, catch him sneaking a meek look in my direction, probably to measure the level of femininity in that woman standing next to him, like most men do, especially when the woman is someone like me: tall and slender. I caught him glancing again, this time at my freshly dyed, loose, luscious hair. He looked away suddenly, like a student who got caught using his phone

---

1 A famous singer (8 October 1959) originally from Syria who spent a huge part of her life in Egypt and sang many popular Egyptian songs

in class, which gave me the chance to further examine his elegant suit jacket and his cravat, which smoothly decorated his white shirt and was styled with a golden pin.

The elevator finally reached its destination. I headed towards the door and would have bumped into him if he hadn't politely gotten out of my way at the last moment. I headed towards my office in a rush, followed by the disapproving stares of the employees, who were certainly thinking, "If this is how the face of our organization behaves, why should we ever be blamed?" Yes, I'm sure they were contemplating how the deputy director of human resources, who never allowed absences or tardiness no matter the excuse, was late herself. I was known for putting up a list that consisted of the names of the employees who were tardy or absent. I decided to add my name to the list to shut them up.

I sat in my office, playing with my pen and thinking about the stranger from the elevator who distracted me with his glances. I estimated that he was nearly ten years older than me; I'm in my mid-thirties and he appeared to be in his mid-forties. He didn't have a ring on his finger just as I didn't have one on mine, but I knew plenty of married men who took off their wedding rings as soon as they got out of their houses, and I didn't rule out the possibility that he could be one of them.

I had a meeting scheduled with one of the employees, who I was meant to investigate due to a complaint issued by his supervisor. The responsibility of investigations was put on my shoulders by the HR director, who gave me most of his tasks and barely showed up himself. He's the CEO's brother, so no one could blame him. If it were up to me, I'd add his name to the weekly list. A secretary came to my office, put a file in front of me, and informed me that it belonged to the head of the new IT department, which surprised me since we didn't have such a department in the first place. We usually resorted to outsourcing IT companies' services without having to employ full-time members. I opened the file in disinterest, but I was quickly taken aback when I found a picture of the man from the elevator inside the file. I learned that he truly was single, and immediately wondered why a man so attractive would still be single, then it occurred to me that he could have been married before then separated, but preferred to keep it as "single" in his papers.

I continued browsing the file and found plenty of certificates, degrees, work experiences, and conferences. He was competent enough to start his own company, so why would he bother to work here in this one? I took a look at his salary and immediately understood his reason when I saw the large amount of money that the company's hiring management was paying him. I continued browsing while pouting my lips in disapproval, judging the CEO's decision to squander this large sum of money on a disposable IT department.

Before I finished examining the file, I suddenly saw him standing right in front of me with a smile on his face. "Good morning, Miss Arwa! I was informed that you're the one in charge of conducting my orientation," he said, which made me so uneasy that I felt the blood rush to my cheeks. I could almost swear that he noticed my nervousness, as his smile got even bigger as if he somehow expected this. I quickly pulled myself together and casually welcomed him aboard, while avoiding eye contact. "Could you please wait for five minutes? I need to quickly get some things done first," I said.

I didn't have any task at hand at the time, but I was desperate to get a grip before I had to accompany that mysterious stranger and give him a workplace tour. I didn't comprehend the reason behind that wave of nervousness and eagerness that overtook me when I was around him, or why I felt like his presence carried endless possibilities. He didn't go easy on me, as he decided to stay with me in my office and wait until I finish the imaginary task I created as an excuse. He seemed comfortable and even asked the office boy to bring him a glass of cold water. I pretended to be focused on the files, yet I still felt his glances examine me and gradually become more courageous, a departure from the reserved glances in the elevator.

I got up and gave him a tour of the office: the rooms, the separated cubicles, and so on. He seemed indifferent about what I was saying and only seemed interested in watching me talk, as he carefully observed my reactions and surrounded me with his stares. Finding that a bit irritating, I decided to initiate a conversation with him, "So, why did you choose to work with us? And what will you further offer than the company that worked with us before?" My words came out sharp and aggressive, but he received them with a composed smile as if he somehow expected my attitude. He noticed I was a strong woman who didn't appreciate being treated in an intimidating way by an older man, so he expected me to protest. We were fighting a subtle, unspoken war against each other.

He responded to my sharp words, "The CEO wanted to create an electronic app and a website to further expand the company's services, and I'm beginning to establish a department where another guy and a girl will work under me."

I sighed in relief as soon as we were done with the office tour. He extended his hand to shake mine, and I gave it to him. He had a firm, yet warm, grip, but he didn't try to let the handshake linger. He acted like a gentleman all the way. Before he walked away, he asked me to be nice to the new guy and girl that were going to work under him. "Everyone says you're too strict, but I beg to differ. Just be gentle with them, they're both fresh grads and can't handle you HR people." He laughed, but it was cut short by my sharp stare.

Less than an hour later, I received a Facebook notification, a request to join the company's group, which was much less active than the dynamic WhatsApp one. The person who sent the request was "Kamel Mahmoud." I accepted the request and opened his profile, only to find normal posts and photos that portrayed the life of a lively man who roamed in many different countries across Europe and Asia. In addition, there were many photos of him on cruises where he went fishing with large groups of men and women in different countries. This online tour of his profile ended up in me sending him a friend request.

I regretted it on the spot and almost canceled the request, but he quickly accepted as if he'd been waiting for it. I felt so angry following my impulsive and meaningless move, I wanted to throw my phone out of the window. My thoughts were interrupted by the employer with whom I was supposed to investigate. I thought to myself that he might be lucky since I was too distracted with everything that took place during the day to focus too much on his issue, but he also might be unfortunate as he arrived at a time where I felt furious at myself. I, however, took a deep breath, attempted to control my feelings, and began to professionally conduct the investigation. I couldn't allow my mood to interfere with my work ethic, as some morons who forbid women from attaining higher-ranking positions claim usually happens.

2

ZIAD—SOUTH PACIFIC OCEAN, APRIL 2010

It was my first hunting trip, but it wasn't exactly what I had always dreamt of. I exerted a huge effort to convince my mom to let me go on a hunting trip on the high seas, but she never allowed it. She claimed that because I hadn't turned ten yet, I wouldn't be able to escape killer whales if they attacked our pod. I swam around her in circles and jumped out of the water ten consecutive times in protest, but she ignored me. I clicked and released the highest-pitched whistles I could emit but to no avail. She insisted that a dolphin had to hunt by the shore for three years and roam around the islands near its shorelines before being competent enough to escape the potential fatal threats he could face in the high seas. I protested again and claimed I swam faster than her, but she responded in the typical, boring wisdom of a mother, "It's not about speed, it's about patience and endurance."

Our small pod headed towards the shallow waters near the coastal area where swarms of fish and anchovies usually swim. I knew that hunting was easy in that area and that anchovies didn't taste so bad, but I was longing to advance from that classification since I had become old enough at that point. My mom, however, was of the anxious kind, who was terrified of letting her kids overcome challenges and obstacles. If I hadn't had enough ambition or desire in me, I would have turned into a meek, tiny, shaky dolphin, like some of my friends who were too scared to hunt without their mothers, even in shallow, danger-free zones.

Maya approached me, steering with her fins and clicking happily. She greeted me before swimming by my side, as we both headed towards the shallow area. Her presence usually brought me great pleasure, making me leap out of the water and spin anytime I spotted her approaching me. On that day, however, I coldly received her. "What's wrong?" she asked me. She sounded worried about me, which I knew from her muffled clicking and her tense fin movement. When I told her the truth, however, she simply belittled my reason, just as I expected. At the end of the day, she was an unambitious girl.

She kept trying to cheer me up, but it didn't work. Eventually, she challenged me to a race, "Let's race to the shallow waters. This time, I will beat you; I've been training well!" she said. That was a smart move, as she knew nothing could get me out of a bad mood more than a race. She swam at her utmost speed, penetrating the water like a sharp arrow, leaping through the air like she would keep flying forever, then returned to the water, which welcomed her back once more. In no time, she'd repeat that same cycle.

I easily surpassed her speed, which made me consider spicing things up a little. I decided to alter my jumping style. I jumped up and bent my tail fluke as much as I could to stir from her right to her left. After I swam past her, I leaped again and spun in a full cycle, while she let out joyful whistles as she tried to dive in deeper to surpass me. I was, however, too busy showing off my moves.

We finally reached the shallow area, where the swarms of anchovies filled the space, waiting for us to feed on them. The process of hunting in that area required a specific set of skills that my mother trained me on. That was my first time, however, to execute them on my own. Some humans on that island would anticipate our arrival and consider it a sign of the presence of large numbers of anchovies, so they would hurriedly throw their nets and steal our food. That's why it is absolutely necessary to be speedy during those times.

There was no time to prepare. Maya and I were in sync as a team, as we rapidly infiltrated the water towards the same group of fish, me from one side and her from the other. When we reached the interface of the group, we dove deeper until we almost hit the seabed and created rings of mud that blinded the smaller fish and led them to move in panic, not knowing where to swim off to. That's when we chose to attack them from every direction. We spun around them in circles, which if a human sees from a higher view, he would think of some galaxies floating in space. Afterwards, one of us would initiate the attack and feed on some of them, then retreat to leave space for the other one to do the same.

The birds seemingly had no clue that there were so many fish in the area. It was as if they were in deep sleep, and only woke up to the noises we released as we devoured our prey. They began to penetrate the water, descending from the skies like shooting stars, and tried to feed on fish from the emptier areas. I clicked and whistled to alert Maya, so she dove in the center of the circle and created a muddiness mist to blind the birds as well, which prevented them from stealing any of our food. This eventually forced them to go hunt somewhere else.

After we grouped up again, we intended to end our trip by a visit to the coast, in a way allowing the smaller fish to attempt to escape before we trap them again. Humans, those tasteless creatures that eradicate everything beautiful in sight, unfortunately, showed up. Whenever we hunted our preys, we made sure we left a sufficient number of them alive to let them reproduce, as my mother had taught me. Humans, however, are short-sighted idiots. When we heard the sound of the very first net being thrown into the water, we turned around and headed back home.

I was feeling much lighter and played around with Maya on our way back. Suddenly, an idea occurred to me. I suggested a game where she would play the role of a prey, while I would play the role of the killer whale (well, in reality, it's not a whale, but a type of a dolphin. Humans, however, insist on calling it a whale, and since the readers of my stories will be human, that's what I will call it as well). And before we could even start to play, Maya stopped, latched on to me, and shifted my attention to a boat nearby. I gently reassured her and we both executed some consecutive high leaps, which greatly impressed the humans on the boat, as they raised their irritating voices in excitement. They assumed we were playing with them; they didn't know we were simply trying to avoid their unexplainable cruelty. After the boat had left peacefully, we calmed down and began to swim side by side back to our pod.

ARWA—CAIRO, MARCH 2017

Two days ago, Kamel and I celebrated our one-month anniversary of meeting for the first time, and today we celebrate the one-month anniversary of our first conversation on Facebook Messenger. During this time, I have been dealing with two entirely different versions of him. The first version was the hard-working, serious engineer, who was adored by his subordinates (unlike me of course) and who only joked around in a restricted manner, in a way that made sure you weren't going to cross any lines with him. He was extremely skilled at what he did, and very protective when it came to the guy and girl who worked directly under him as if they were some sort of personal responsibility. He denied my right to criticize or penalize them, even though I was completely authorized to do so as the deputy HR director.

The second version of Kamel was the man who opened up his heart to me, but only in the virtual world. He was a father who missed his kids as they lived abroad in Dubai with their mother, a vivacious person who was tortured by a sense of solitude, an avid reader who read about diverse topics, and an expert in women, or so he claimed. Ever since he and his wife were separated, he went through many romantic adventures with women,both here in Egypt and abroad. He told me myriads of stories, where each woman left her impact and signboard in the streets of his heart; a heart which felt to me like a large city, as vast as Cairo or Rome.

In the beginning, I insisted that we remain only friends. I told him I wasn't going to allow our conversations to surpass the non-platonic zones and he easily accepted. In fact, it was too easy to an extent that aggravated me. He was a gentleman and a good listener, and I specifically admired the way he tried to view the problems I told him about from a woman's perspective. It was as if he could read all women's minds. What attracted me even more and allowed me to let my guard down, is how much he unapologetically expressed his emotions and was never too embarrassed to show his weaknesses or flaws. One time we had a video call (which resembled a normal real-life conversation, like we were sitting together somewhere in public), and he shared a personal story about a close friend of his who used to work with him in a large company in Dubai. Before working together, their friendship had continued for more than ten years. One day, Kamel discovered a large violation that his friend had secretly committed, and he found himself in an unfortunate position where he was forced to report it. However, he preferred to inform his friend about it so as not to stab him in the back.

He didn't care for his friend's pleas, as he was disappointed in him and scared to lose his job at the same time. When they found out about the violation at their workplace, it was a large scandal that left a black mark on his friend's clean record and shut the doors of his ever working in Dubai for good. The man coincidentally had an instant heart attack that ended his life before he even turned forty. Years later, Kamel still bore the guilt of his friend's death. Tears slid down his face as he told me the story, so he tried to end the call or turn it into a voice call instead, but I refused. I had an overwhelming desire to stay by his side to somewhat ease his pain. By the end of the call, he told me that my words indeed had that kind of powerful effect on him, and in his own words, consoled the deepest pits of his soul.

That conversation was a turning point in our relationship, as it upgraded our friendship into some kind of a concealed, unspoken love. After that, he admitted that he also felt like he was dealing with two versions of me: the first one was Arwa, referred to as "grumpy Madam Mervat[2] from Human resources department" by everyone at work, a nickname that I had no idea about but that cracked me up at the same time as it perfectly summarized my work mode. The second version is Arwa, the childlike, motherly, and ladylike Arwa all at once. He would always call me "my lady," in English, whenever he texted me first thing in the morning, or right before he went to bed. He'd also insist that I was only missing a

---

[2] A well-known Egyptian cultural reference that jokingly makes fun of grumpy older women who work as government employees or civil servants and like to give everyone a hard time

dress from the previous century and a vintage hand fan to look like a princess from the royal family of Mohamed Aly's[3], fresh out of Abdeen Palace[4].

He slowly conquered my heart. Every time I built a protective wall around it, he would never try to break it down; instead, he would swerve to move past it, in a way that resembled a peaceful stream rather than an overwhelming flood. It was the kind of stream, however, whose water generously and constantly flowed. I had built plenty of protective walls, due to my previous struggles with the rough opposite gender, and by *rough* here I'm not only indicating their appearances but their hearts and souls as well.

My ex-husband was on the top of that list. He was distant and cautious with both his feelings and his money, even though he was an attractive and well-off gentleman who graduated from the American University in Cairo, where our relationship was a source of envy to my colleagues. Back then, I didn't think that romantic love should be the foundation upon which a relationship is built. Instead, I believed that love was going to flourish on its own with time, as long as I picked a compatible partner. I thought I could easily make him fall in love with me, simply because I'm good-looking and fun. After months had passed, any desire I once had of a romantic

---

[3] The Albanian Ottoman governor and the de facto ruler of Egypt from 1805 to 1848, who is considered the founder of modern Egypt

[4] A historic Cairo palace which was built as one of the official residences for the former ruling monarchy and royal family of Egypt. It is now a museum located in Abdeen, Cairo.

relationship disappeared into thin air. He never shared a word of love with me, and I never caught a spark of emotion in his eyes. It was a purely mechanical marriage, even during its utmost intimate aspects, which resembled procedural movements that were similar to a computer's response to presses on its keyboard. Even computers sometimes produce heat when you give them some important order that speeds up its fan, unlike that man who stole a year and a half of my life.

After my divorce, I tried to alter my perspective of love by making it the center of my next potential relationship. Again, I was naïve, but in a different way. I was like a fool who attempted to move an elephant from its place by pushing it desperately from behind, and when that failed, I tried to drag it with a rope. Of course, an elephant would only move of its own free will when it desired to eat, not at any other random time.

Kamel, however, was a different story. He wasn't an elephant, but a graceful horse that loved to roam and run whether there was grass around or not, disregarding life's limitations or restrictions. On the day of the one-month anniversary of our first conversation, he asked to meet me at night. Of course, it was a non-work-related meeting. I made my hesitance clear before agreeing, and I wasn't playing "hard to get"; it was a genuine reluctance. Of course, I wanted to meet him outside the company. I wanted to go out with the Kamel who I'd been bonding with on Facebook, not the version that stirs up trouble at work if I penalize one of his subordinates. However, it was still a big step that carried a lot of questions we hadn't answered yet.

Eventually, I cut my reluctance short and agreed to meet with him. He said he was going to pass by my house, but I asked him to choose a place where we could meet instead. He then told me to head to "Bayt Al-Suhaymi[5]" in Al-Moez street[6]. I pondered that suggestion on my way there, wondering why he would specifically choose that place, which was a 350-year-old house that hosted formal events sometimes. I wondered if he planned for us to attend some poetry recital night or a musical show, or one of those similar events I couldn't stand.

I stood in front of the vertical mirror in my room, watching myself in different outfits and trying to pick the right color and style. Eventually, I settled on an outfit that I had bought two months ago and completely forgotten about, yet it saved me on that particular day. It subtly showed off my moderately curvy figure and concealed some of its flaws, which weren't that obvious to begin with.

I stood in front of my bathroom mirror to figure out what I should do about my face. My long, jet-black hair generally reassured me, even though some of it had been falling off lately. My wide, dark eyes are a bit slanted in a way that many women wish for, despite that minor puffiness in my lower left eyelid, which has become more apparent when I use makeup and which forces me to take a longer time to paint them.

---

[5] An Islamic-themed house and museum in Cairo, Egypt, originally built in 1648

[6] It is one of Cairo's oldest streets as it dates back to the foundation of the city by the Fatimid dynasty in the tenth century, under their fourth caliph, Al-Mu'izz li-Din Allah

I contemplated my straight, sharp nose with its soft, rounded tip, but that was covered with pores which I could luckily conceal with foundation. My cheeks are rounded, but again, with some effort, I could make them appear more contoured like models' cheeks. My lips are full, but they needed a suitable red tint. I wasn't planning on overlining them in a way that would give a false impression of them being oversized, they were naturally full enough.

When I finally arrived, Kamel was standing right in front of the door. He received my hand in a way that filled my whole body with warmth, even though it wasn't the first time I shook his hand. He pushed the richly ornamented wooden door and we ended up at the house's courtyard after crossing a narrow passage. It was my first time there! He took me by the hand like a child and began to enthusiastically explain the stories behind things I saw without realizing their true value.

There was a band playing in the courtyard opposite the small garden. "Are they having an event?" I asked. He smiled and responded, "They are, but it's to celebrate you, my lady." I opened my mouth in astonishment, so he said, "Simply enjoy the night, and try not to ask too many questions." He took me on a tour of the place, while I followed his lead, like a student who followed her mentor or a child who followed her father and openly received all the information she was given. I would glance at a wall and he would instantly explain its design, style, and what has been written about it, so my eyes would open to see a new kind of beauty for the first time.

"The ladies' reception!" he said as we entered a large courtyard with decorative and colorful marble. It seemed like a space for women's gossiping sessions at the time. From there, we walked into another space, which he claimed to be a "ladies' hall." He then took me on a tour recounting the events that took place there centuries ago, and after, he stood me in front of a "mashrabiya window[7]," opened it, and asked me to wait there. "Promise me you will keep looking down at the hall bellow." I promised and waited in anticipation, while curiosity ate at me to find out what would happen next. I then saw him waiting below the mashrabiya window, waving his hand and throwing a flower at me. I grabbed it, smelled it, and laughed till tears rolled down my cheeks at his teenage-like behavior, not believing any of what was going on.

We continued the tour, during which that warm, loving feeling never left me for a second. It was a feeling that I was around a man who pampered me, cared for me, and saved me the trouble of thinking about the next step. Some might call me an exaggerator for saying what I'm about to say, but it was a feeling even more beautiful than love. Maybe I was stupid to think so because a feeling like this wouldn't be complete without love, but the truth is, love itself wouldn't be complete if it didn't have what I felt at that moment with Kamel.

He took me to the last station, a large balcony that looked upon the courtyard, where we could see the

---

[7] A type of projecting oriel window enclosed with carved wood latticework located on the upper floors of a building, it is characteristic of traditional architecture in the Islamic world

musical band that had already started playing. They were playing a specific song by Mayada Al-Hennawy that I'd already told him I love. The balcony accommodated an upper level which had a rug with a copper high tray on it, and behind that setting, there was Arabesque wood. He asked me to sit by it before he called out for a waiter who appeared in modern clothes that contrasted with the appearance of the place. He began to serve us our dinner, which included all the recipes I told him were my favorite during the times we chitchatted about our days. I didn't picture I was going to sit on the ground to have my dinner, but a table would have taken away from the magic of the moment. As we had dinner, the band was playing in a beautiful ode-like way, to complete the picture and add to a fascinating night I never dared to dream about in my most optimistic dreams.

ZIAD—SOUTH PACIFIC OCEAN 2012

After two years of swimming in shallow waters exclusively, I was finally allowed to go on a hunting trip on the high seas. My mother was still opposed to the idea, but the leader of our pod insisted that any dolphin that exceeded two years of independent hunting had to join the trip. The exploring dolphins (which are dolphins specifically trained in exploring fish swarms in deep zones) were certain that there was a large swarm of lanternfish in a distance that would take us around a full day and night of traveling to reach.

Our pod set out on its long journey. We were swimming at a medium speed while dancing on the surface level and jumping in sync, like we were on an exciting picnic. Everything we did was for fun, including our long and exhausting hunting journeys. No one in his right mind would assume that thousands of us dolphins gather and travel all this way just to feed. Lanternfish isn't even that tasty, but the thrill of a challenge and an exciting trip was the real source of pleasure to us.

Maya's slow speed hindered us, always keeping the two of us behind the rest, which I didn't enjoy. She suggested, with her usual intelligence, that we dive deeper into the water to join the lower line of dolphins. Swimming with them is easier, but it requires that we elevate ourselves every once in a while, to be able to take a breath, which was of course going to hinder both of us. Yet I listened to her anyway.

We plunged into the deeper level of water, where I was surprised to spot a long swarm of golden tuna fish. They were irritating and meddlesome, clinging to our pod and trying to steal our prey. They were simply an inferior species that didn't have many skills besides intruding on us. I approached them and let out an annoying whistle while splashing my fins, which terrified them. Maya swam to join me, protesting with some angry clicks, "Let them be! Why do you bother them? Do you think that the millions of fish that await us belong to us only? Don't act like a stupid human!"

I could almost feel the water around me boil with rage, so I said, "How dare you insult me and compare me to a stupid human?" She ignored my protest and went her way, so I set out at my rapid speed and left her in the dust, still making sure I was within the range of her sound waves so she could still sense where I was and follow me. I picked a certain spot and powerfully thrust my tail, heading out like a speedy rocket that went off among the lines of dolphins. I leaped high in the air, surpassing both the bigger and smaller fish while spinning with my body. Then I dove down into the water, swerving left and right to avoid the large number of dolphins, until I eventually reached the deeper lines again.

Maya joined me once more. "You misunderstood me! I didn't mean to compare you to a stupid human, I just meant that you think like one when you believe that we own the whole ocean. You're not more deserving of food just because you're smarter than tuna!" she told me.

One of the older dolphins came to us and ordered me to join the group in the deepest levels. I almost jumped with joy, since I knew it was a task assigned to only the most skilled and experienced dolphins. I said goodbye to Maya and joined the dolphins in those levels, where we were supposed to determine the location of the lanternfish with our sounds. It was a swarm the size of a large island, which meant they represented a generous meal for us and that the tuna fish, and even birds, could join the feast when we drive those fish to the surface level.

A large group—the size of an island—of small fish was swimming in all directions in calm harmony and at a slow pace. We swam beneath them, causing fear and chaos, which led them to swim up to the surface. It looked like an entire island floating above us as if one of the seamounts below got fed up with the darkness down there and decided to rise to the surface and enjoy the sunlight. All the creatures began to feed, catching tens of fish at a time. The scene resembled tiny rice grains getting hurled into one large, hungry mouth. I left the group at the bottom, which was responsible for forbidding the lanternfish from re-escaping down to the bottom, and headed towards Maya, relying on the special whistles we shared to find where she was. After we were done feeding, we swam around for a while watching the tuna fish devour our leftovers. After that, the majestic whiptail stingray fish arrived. They resembled birds with massive wings or stealth aircraft, except that whiptail stingrays moved their wings in a flowy manner. They showed up in a structure that looked like a group of aircrafts forming an arrowhead that penetrated any fish that came their way and devoured whichever kind they desired.

Maya leaned on me and said jokingly, "See? We all get to eat, the food isn't going anywhere. The fish is still always going to be available in great numbers, and they will mate and bring new generations to life!"

"You're right, I did behave like a stupid human, I won't do that again," I told her, to which she said, "I know you well, and I know how kind you are at heart. That's why I only go hunting with you." I felt joyful goosebumps take over my entire body from tale to snout, "And that's why I only accompany you in all my activities, not just hunting!" I replied.

I noticed that the whiptail stingrays were finally done feeding on the swarm of small fish, more than half of which remained alive. They gathered themselves and swam together towards the bottom of the ocean once again as if they were offering part of their flock as a sacrifice so the circle of life could carry on in a perfect system. That is unless, of course, humans interfere and mess with this balance, disrupting the entire equation. "Lucky for us and for those fish that they reside in the bottom of the ocean, where they can't be hunted by humans. That way, they still provide their bountiful blessings without running out!" I told Maya.

ARWA—CAIRO, APRIL 2018

Fasting can make food seem more delicious than it actually is! Ever since I first started fasting Ramadan[8] as a little girl, I found refraining from food to be extremely challenging. I remember one time my mother was emptying bags of vegetables when a cucumber fell on the kitchen floor and my mother forgot to pick it back up. I took the cucumber and intended to give it back to her when something strange suddenly happened! The cucumber transformed in my head: from a dull, tasteless vegetable that tasted like nothing but fibers mixed with water, to a delightful fruit with a strong smell that melted inside my brain convolutions, melting it in return. I cut it in half and practically drooled when I noticed its juice, which truly has no taste at all, and how it resembled fat melting off a steak that is getting slowly grilled. Its green peel, which I refused to swallow before, was calling out for

[8] The ninth month of the Islamic calendar, observed by Muslims worldwide as a month of fasting, prayer, reflection, and community.

me like "El-Naddaha[9]," so I had to follow its hypnotizing voice. When I eventually decided to eat the cucumber, only the first bite tasted good. When I had my second bite, it went back to tasting like dull fibers mixed with water, but I had already broken my long, hard fast for it.

After that first date I had with Kamel, I was scared to think that it might be similar to that initial tasty bite of the cucumber, and then he would go back to being a regular man, a wolf in a sheep's clothing. I felt responsible for protecting my heart, as I wondered what I was doing to it and to which path I was dragging it along with me. All roads were bumpy, sloping, and led to deep valleys. I was never a pessimistic or cynical woman. On the contrary, I always insisted on remaining a source of hope and optimism. After my divorce, I optimistically awaited love to knock on my door; the kind of love that had no limits or conditions. Every man I met, however, offered nothing but shallow and naïve feelings. It didn't matter how or where I met them, be it someone I met at work, in the sporting club, or through the virtual world. My feelings towards them always resembled my experience with that one cucumber: the first bite was tasty, and then the same combination of tasteless water mixed with fibers took over.

I spent the entire night tossing and turning in bed. During my long sleepless night, I realized that the main reason behind my anxiety was that Kamel still hadn't expressed his feelings for me yet. What if he just wanted

---

[9] A mythical creature and a modern legend, surrounding the story of female naiad-like genies who call men to the Nile's water, most likely to their deaths

to fool around? What if he was one of those men who enjoyed watching the look of bedazzlement in a woman's eyes, but then that was it? What if, after he finally achieved his goal, he simply asked me to get off stage so he could choose his new spectator?

The next morning, I went to work with a pallid face. In my office, I found the file of an employee who submitted a request to take a couple of days off to stay with her sick mother. I almost automatically denied her request due to how bitter I felt, but I held back at the very last moment. I opened one of my drawers and found an envelope with the words, "Attn: Miss Arwa, confidential and private" written on it. I thought to myself, "Great, exactly what I needed! A letter from the State Security Investigations," but as soon as I began to read the contents of the letter, my heart almost stopped beating.

> "To her Ladyship/Miss Arwa,
>
> I wanted to hand you this letter last night myself, but my shyness prevented me from doing that. You might find this strange since I'm normally not a timid person, but you were responsible for adding this quality to my operating system ever since you started intervening in my personal software. Excuse the lame metaphor, but this is the hundred and twentieth time that I attempt to write a letter good enough for you,

and I had sworn that this would be the last one no matter how it turned out to be. No letter could possibly convey the intensity of my feelings. I love you … that's what I've been wanting to say and found extremely difficult to utter when I was with you. I also thought that you are way above learning this via typewritten words on a screen, so no, I wanted you to read it in my handwriting and to see, through the curvature of the letters my hand wrote, some of the feelings that flow within my heart.

Dear Lady Arwa,

I wish I could write, "My love," but "my" indicates some sort of possession that I don't have access to until I know how you feel towards me. Only you can bless me with the right to add the word "my" when I want to refer to you. Therefore, I ask you to let me know—vocally, in written form, or digital form—whether I have the right to say it or not.

Sincerely,
Kamel"

That was how the letter that made my hands shake and made me lose control of myself, came to an end. It was the second bite that turned out to be even more delicious and filling than the first one. Contemplating how to respond, I got up, headed to the bathroom, stood in front of the mirror to pull myself together, then returned to my office. There, I found the employee with the vacation request waiting for me. I picked up the paper and signed it without thinking, as she couldn't believe her own eyes in a way that almost drove her to tears. I, however, cut off the series of praise she was letting at me and asked her to leave. I got out a piece of paper and started writing.

> "To the respectable engineer, Mr. Kamel
>
> In response to the query in your letter, and after consulting with the stakeholders, I'm pleased to inform you that I don't at all mind that you apply the suggested pronoun to refer to me. In fact it would be my pleasure.
>
> Sincerely,
> Arwa"

I folded the letter, put it in an envelope and wrote on it, "Attn: Mr. Kamel, confidential and private." I sent it to him while ignoring all my fears as if I had already intended to drag my feet to a risky adventure with an undetermined ending. Minutes later, I was surprised to receive a text message from him, "You still didn't reply!"

My fingers were about to start typing but I stopped myself. I decided to ignore that message since he was being too greedy. I responded to his letter, but he still insisted on receiving a very specific reply. I told myself that I was going to ignore him, that I wasn't going to submit that quickly. However, my fingers started writing a response despite myself.

"I did reply. You're allowed to use the word you asked about, I don't mind"

"I meant you didn't reply to 'I love you'"

"Give me ten minutes, I need to get some work done first"

I left our conversation, got rid of my hesitance, took a deep breath, and finally decided to move forward, leaving all my fears behind. I looked for the lyrics of one song that kept playing in my head. I downloaded the song, picked the verse I wanted, then sent it to him in a message and wrote the lyrics underneath it.

"He said I love you, I said it back ... a word requited between two hearts

The flowers danced, the moon shone, a breeze sang alongside two lovebirds

My love loves me back ... is there anything better than that[10]?"

His reply to my message was, "I'm dying to sit with you right now, I have so much to say." I didn't know

---

10 The lyrics of an Egyptian song, sung by Samira Saiid, called "My love loves me back"

how to respond, so I settled for sending him that smiling face emoji, the one with the reserved smile. The screen then showed that he was typing, typing, and typing some more. He took such a long time typing that message, and in the end, I received a text that only consisted of different shapes of kissing emojis that completely took over our whole conversation's screen.

He asked to meet after work, but I refused. The rushing of events already felt overwhelming, especially since just the night before, I could barely sleep from fear and overthinking. The morning after, I'm confessing my love to him. Now, he wants to meet me, and I wouldn't exclude the possibility that he might want to hold my hand in front of people to show off our commitment to one another, the same one that was imaginary or uncertain just a couple of hours ago.

When I went to my parents' house to have lunch with them, happiness took over my entire face despite the on-and-off fits of anxiety I had. My parents lived ten minutes away from me. After my divorce, my mother insisted that I live with them again, but I stubbornly refused. My father accepted my decision, like he always did since I was a kid. My mother kept asking me, as she often did, about my love life and if there was some potential husband on the way. She asked that question at least twice a week, like a typical mother who wished for nothing but her daughter's marriage, even though she worked as a doctor, had a master's degree, and attended plenty of conferences with Westerners, who she worked and dealt with all the time.

Later that evening, I met up with Naglaa on the sporting club's track. Our work conditions forced us to always work out at night. I opened up to her about my relationship with Kamel, recounting the story while trying to catch my breath from the speed of our jogging and the excessive excitement. "Hold on, let's sit! This deserves my full attention," Naglaa told me, so we sat down at a table. She ordered a latte while I ordered green tea. "Careful! You're about to regain all the calories you just burned if you drink that creamy foam covering your coffee," I said. "Well, I need to stay focused if I'm giving you my advice," she replied.

She was shocked to learn that Kamel was able to rent a historical place and host an entire dinner in my honor. "His cousin has a high-ranking job in the ministry of antiquities, according to him," I informed her. She thought about it and said, "This whole thing is too good to be true. It's like the kind of romance we see in movies. This perfection could be a bit pretentious, but that's just a thought." Disappointment took over my face as I said, "You just killed my excitement." She then swore and swore that she didn't mean to invalidate his feelings, but she wanted me to carefully enter his world, to not give out my heart for free, and to always consider the possibility that what's on the surface doesn't necessarily indicate what's in the bottom. She then finished her words of advice saying, "However, a man as handsome and rich as he is wouldn't exert all that effort just to fool around. I'm sure he has feelings for you, but you still need to take it slowly, one day at a time." I took the last sip in my cup and thought to myself, "let us simply enjoy the moment, and leave the abstract details to God."

ARWA—CAIRO, MAY 2018

For two whole days, I refused to meet him outside of work, until I woke up on the third day and decided to liberate my feelings and let go of my fear. I decided to cautiously store my fear in a tiny, velvet box and shut it without locking it all the way. After all, it is much safer to leave a small gap open for my fears to escape than to lock them up completely, which is quite risky.

Strangely, he wrote another handwritten letter to me on that same day. In the morning, I woke up to knocks on my door, and it turned out to be the delivery boy from a courier service, who carried a small parcel in his hand. I took it from him, opened the parcel, and found a book about the "art of life" or something of the sort. Attached to its cover was a carefully folded paper. I opened it and found a message from Kamel written on it.

"My beloved Arwa, my wonderful lady ..." I immediately thought to myself, "There we go, a Nizar

Qabbani[11] reference!" but I continued reading the letter anyway.

"I love you, Arwa! As someone who works with codes and defined numbers, it is challenging for me to reach such a sentimental conclusion … especially that this word 'love' existed before in my life, but now its definition has become vague.

Love is an indefinite word in my dictionary, I can't find a specific meaning or scientific standard for it. I did, however, wake up one day to the realization that I love you, just like one knows when he's feeling happy, sad, or angry. I know that the heart is just a strong organ that pumps blood, I know that feelings reside in the convolutions of the brain and they're more of electrical impulses like the ones we have on our computers, which I'm familiar with. Yet I can swear that I physically feel my heart dance between my ribs when I hear your voice or see your face and that I feel it break and crack when it feels your pain or distress for whichever reason. Not only that, but you have been taking over everything in my life. My lady, you have become the noises that fill my mornings, the serenity of my nights, and the rhythm of my life. You represent the details forming inside me and around me, the smile that covers my lips, the critical thinking that leaves a frown on my forehead, the cup of coffee I drink, my keyboard, my programming codes that carry images and music similar to the music of my love to you, which is carried within all those details. If I were a bird, you'd

---

[11] A Syrian poet and writer (21 March 1923 – 30 April 1998) known for his romantic, contemporary poems

be the tree that keeps me safe, and I would have stayed in the protection of your arms day and night. If I were a sailor, I would have camped in the ports of your eyes. If I were anything in the world, I would have chosen to be a part of you, like you have become part of me."

I folded the letter, called Kamel, and asked him how he was able to formulate and express his feelings that way. He shyly responded, "I read something a while ago that had a similar meaning, but I wrote it in my own way. I picked from it what I thought matched my feelings as you did before with that song."

We met later that night. He picked me up with his car, we had dinner, walked a little, then rode in his car again. He grabbed my hand, put it on his mouth, and kissed it, in a way that I have never been kissed. My facial features were shivering and my face turned pale. It was a kiss on the palm of my hand, but I felt it flow all over my body. I didn't utter a word until I finally arrived at my house and we spent the entire night texting. I asked him what was the reason behind his kiss, he told me that the main and most important reason is that it was from the heart and that his lips and the palm of my hand were just methods to convey what's inside the heart. He then added, "Hand kisses have different meanings, and the way I kissed tonight is to express passionate love, especially if it's done how I did it, with a half-open mouth." I let out a loud laugh and I added many laughing emojis in my text, but he swore it was the truth. I asked, "So you have never kissed someone that way before?" to which he said that he always did it with closed lips and that I was the first woman he kissed with a half-open mouth.

If a friend of mine was describing that conversation to me, I would call her a fool and let her know that she fell into a trap of a man who's good with words. On that day, however, I decided to put all my fears behind and let myself enjoy every word, gesture, and joke. I asked myself, "What's the point of stressing out?" and the answer was nothing but ruining that pleasant moment.

I began to behave differently at work. I frowned less, became more open, and the pleasant feeling of new love had obsecured every other feeling. I soared up in a different sky from everyone else, and occasionally landed to visit my fellow humans and deal with their problems, then went back to fly in my own sky again. My looks at Kamel almost exposed me! When I ran into him in the corridor of the office, my face lit up and flowers bloomed on my lineaments. I thought everyone noticed that.

My boss summoned me one day, and I suddenly felt like the ground was about to swallow me open. I had a sure feeling that he was going to talk to me about my relationship with Kamel, perhaps warn about how it had become a source of gossip in the office, or advise me against going out with him due to how it might affect my reputation. Even worse, I was scared he might tell me information about Kamel that would destroy the perfect image that I drew of him. One of the downsides of getting into a great relationship is your constant, excessive fear that it will get ruined. Nothing scares you when you are feeling empty or when you're in a shaky relationship, but when the love of your life shows up in the picture, it makes you think that everything around is trying to destroy that magical happiness you're living, or that one day, an unexpected wake-up call will show up and tell you that has been an illusion all along.

Fortunately, my boss wanted to speak to me about something unrelated to Kamel. He was letting me know that I have become too lenient with the employees and that it has been lately making him uncomfortable, since he was used to using me as a disciplinary method with the lazy employees instead of blaming it on the management itself. Usually, an employee would go to him to complain about my strictness, so my boss would promise to try and fix things. "You know what Miss Arwa is like! She is authorized by the board of directors! And Mr. Ahmed, the head of HR, is usually absent, so I can't intervene with her decisions. But I promise I will try to talk to her," he would tell him.

I always knew what he had just told me, but it never occurred to me that he told the employees I was personally supported by the board of directors and that my supervisor himself couldn't control my actions. All of that was nonsense of course and there was no one to blame but the employee who believed that. I didn't try to elongate our discussion any further, but I promised that I was going to go back to being my usual, strict self. He then repeated his irrational words about the board of directors and how they provided me with authorities that even he couldn't overstep, telling me that he wished I used this power in a way that benefitted the company.

I met with Kamel more frequently, around two or three times a week, during which our bond evolved, our talks became smoother and our lives intermingled amazingly. One evening, as we sat together in an outdoor restaurant in "Al Masa[12]" garden while a band played oriental tunes, I was talking to him about a random subject that isn't even worth mentioning, when he suddenly interrupted me with a serious look on his face. "I want to ask for your hand in marriage," he said.

Ever since we started going out, I was expecting him to take this step at any moment. Sometimes I would get nervous thinking about it, wondering if he was just having meaningless fun or simply wasting my time. I expected a grand, romantic gesture, like the ones we see in movies or on TV. I pictured him bringing a large cake with a surprise ring inside it, or a set of balloons with the words "Marry Me" written on it or something of the sort. After all, he's an extremely romantic man and was expected to propose romantically. My happiness with his proposal, however, won me over and made me forget about my desire to be proposed to in a Western style.

"You should ask me first before you ask my parents! What if I say no?" I said, with a playful smile. He smiled back and said, "Dreamers like me can only follow their hearts." He extended his hand to hold mine, so I smiled timidly and didn't add anything. "I do, however, have one little request, and I hope it doesn't bother you," he said. My heart sank in my chest as a strong wave of nervousness and bad expectations took over me. I thought about a million potential scenarios to what he was going to ask from me, and I suddenly assumed that he hid many unpleasant surprises that he finally decided to confront me with.

---

[12] A lavish and luxurious hotel surrounded by landscaped gardens in Cairo, Egypt

ARWA—CAIRO, MAY 2018

I always believed that every perfect package had secret layers within it that could easily disfigure its perfection. There was no way a man with such raw emotions, delightful presence, and fiery passion didn't drag along something that was able to stain that delightful fountain that exploded with honey and wine.

He asked me to keep the news of our marriage limited to our family and closest friends and to avoid spreading the news among people at work for the time being. He wanted to wait for a year or a year and a half at most before we could tell everyone and begin planning to start a family. Even though maternal instincts usually take over any woman, especially a woman my age who was in the middle of her reproductive years or at the beginning of their second phase, those instincts bowed down to the heat of love that Kamel overwhelmed me with and behind my strong desire to find the perfect love.

The idea of motherhood never mattered to me as much as finding love did. I always believed that perfect love, on its own, is the most satisfying, overpowering, and wonderful feeling. However, this feeling is lacking if it doesn't have three things: a sense of stability, which is usually a result of marriage; the feeling of pleasure, which is the result of a physical relationship with your partner; and the state of motherhood, which is a result of becoming a parent (which is another experience on its own, with a method, purpose, and result). No matter how idealistic a relationship is, no matter how much it's filled with poems, letters, love gazes, and longing, it remains fragile if one of those basic aspects didn't exist within it. At least, that's how I viewed things as a woman in my thirties, and I'm unsure if it will change again with age. When I was a teenager, love to me was nothing more significant than a flower that someone put in my book or a song that someone sent me.

Kamel's reason behind his request wasn't convincing to me! He swore that most of his money existed as financial investments in Dubai under his wife's authority, as they were all written under her name during their marriage to make things easier. When they got divorced, she acknowledged that the money was his and promised she was going to give it to him through installments, but she kept stalling. The main problem was that her friend's husband, a friend of Kamel himself, warned him that she was worried about Kamel getting married and having kids. In that case, his kids would share her daughters' inheritance; coincidentally, she intended to make as much profit as she could from his money before returning it to him. She swore that if he did ever get married, he wasn't going to get his money in any way, justifying that by the fact that he earned a lot at his job and that he had other savings as well.

"Maybe she still loves you and wants to get back with you, so she's using money as an excuse," I said with a serious face, while avoiding eye contact and distracting myself by tossing my spoon in what was left of my soufflé. "She's incapable of loving anyone but herself, as I told you before," he replied with a begging voice. He swore that everything he once told me about the hideousness of living with that woman was true, that what he had endured during the past three years for his kids was above anyone's capabilities and that he left Dubai and came to live in Cairo just to be away from her, even if it meant not being able to see his kids.

At that moment, an energy strong enough to kill any sympathy had taken over my heart, but he wouldn't stop begging and swearing, to the extent that his eyes teared up in a way that caught people's attention. I told him I wanted to leave and got up to take a cab, but he insisted he would drive me home himself, which I thought wouldn't do any harm. I wanted to stay by myself at home so I could think clearly. When we got into his car, he still wouldn't stop repeating the same words over and over. He begged, swore, and pledged his love for me while cursing the unfair timing that made him meet me at a later stage. I sarcastically said, "When you got married to her, I was still a kid." He swore that if he had met me then, he would have waited for me to grow older until it became appropriate for us to get married.

At that moment, an idea nagged at me like none other. I wondered if he meant to drown me in his love, passion, and excessive romance until he made sure I became too attached to him in a way that made leaving him too painful. After that, there could be no way out of this. I wondered if this was all a staged play, and that me accepting his offer would be one of its acts, while the rest of the upcoming acts included me compromising in many other different ways.

While he was driving, he was still crying and expressing his love. He unleashed the tears that he kept to himself earlier when we were still in the garden, and by the time we arrived at my house, he was sobbing like a little kid. He told me, "The only thing I've been praying to God for is to have you and that's it. I'm not asking for too much! It's just one year as if we're engaged and getting married in a year." I responded in a flat voice, "The problem is that you kept all of this from me. How do I know that everything you did before wasn't to make sure you have me under your control so I could sign up for something I don't want? Come on, aren't you the same person who rented a historical place in honor of our first date?" He said, "All my life I dreamed about having someone to share such beautiful moments with until I found you and chose to live all my dreams with you. The ecstasy I feel when I see your happiness always exceeds your happiness itself. I did everything because I love you and because I wanted to fill a hole that you and only you could fill."

His words and tears touched me. I knew it didn't make sense for a man to break down that way in front of a woman who he only wanted to waste his time with, or who he wanted to marry for his personal gains. Ever since I met Kamel, he made sure I never worried about anything. He never tried to prove his manhood with control or overstated promises, but he always proved it with actions, sophistication, and respect for my beliefs and ideas, even if some of them were a bit shallow or basic. I always knew I had traits that could trigger some men to try to own me or want to be with me, but I don't think any woman could have any quality that could make a man sob like a child in front of her unless he loves her. I contemplated how love had to include compassion, forgiveness, and understanding, especially knowing that he was probably scared of my reaction if he told me about this problem from the beginning.

I asked him to give me some time to think about it. When I was alone in my bedroom, I called Naglaa and told her the full story. "You have no reason to be mad!" she said. "The man could've proposed and then delayed the actual marriage for a year until his situation becomes stable, but he didn't. A one-year engagement period isn't that long despite what some people think, even if you're a divorcee, but he decided to spend it married to you anyway. The guy can't wait, he's dying to marry you. I'm this close to asking you to leave him to me, I can leave my husband and marry him!" Her words didn't calm me down, as I felt like our conversation was becoming less serious than it should have been. Therefore, I decided to reach out to an old friend, Moemen, whose opinion I deeply trusted, especially since he supported me during my post-divorce period. I thought that a man's opinion in that matter could make more sense, and honestly, his words truly did comfort me and eventually led me to accept Kamel's request.

Kamel asked me not to tell the full details of his story to my father, as he intended to convince him in his own way, which I hesitantly accepted. During his meeting with my parents, when he was asking for my hand in marriage, Kamel told my father about the problems he had with his ex-wife that forced him to announce the news of our marriage to our family only for the first year. My father didn't object as long as I didn't have problems with this. "Normally, I don't ask for too much when it comes to bridewealth or wedding gifts. Three of my daughters have already gotten married, and I learned that this whole matter goes back to the groom and his situation. But in your case of requesting to keep the marriage unannounced for some time, my standards will be different since I want to guarantee my daughter's rights!" my father said.

My father asked him for half a million Egyptian pounds as a bridewealth, but he didn't determine a specific value for the wedding gift and left it to Kamel's estimation, since it's supposed to be a gift from the groom. Moreover, my father asked for an additional million pounds as deferred alimony. I thought my father's requests were extremely exaggerated, that he was resorting back to his rural ideologies or rituals since he asked for such a large amount. Kamel, however, actually accepted all his conditions and even claimed that if it were up to him, he would double up all those numbers. Later, they read "Al Fatiha[13]" together and settled on a day to consummate the marriage contract.

---

[13] A Muslim custom that involves the reading of the first chapter of the Quran (titled Al Fatiha) in the presence of the new married

The following day, I found an envelope in my office. I opened it and found an intimate letter with a sincere apology written in it, plus a car key that was explained to be my wedding gift. Filled with curiosity, I immediately left the office and found the car parked in a garage two streets away from the company. It was a Korean, reasonably priced Kia Soul which had a stylish color and appearance. It made the process of getting rid of my previous car extremely doable. I opened the car door and began to check it out carefully, only to find him opening the opposite door and greeting me. I stepped back in shock, as my heart almost stopped from the surprise. He was wearing an elegant suit, different from the one he wore at the office, and a chic cravat. With a smile on his face, he got a small box out of his pocket and opened it to reveal a white-gold ring with a small diamond stone on it. He sweetly whispered, "Will you marry me?"

I laughed and said, "This is too much!" to which he responded, "Not for you." I then asked, "Do you really love me?" He nodded his head and swore that he did. He then grabbed my hand and began to slide the ring down my finger, so I said, "What's that?" I never said "Yes" or "I do" or any of the words that should be said. He kissed the palm of my hand with a half-open mouth, looking at me imploringly, to which I nodded, and let him put the ring on my finger as my heart continued to flutter.

---

couple to be with their immediate family and sometimes extended relatives

ZIAD—SOUTH PACIFIC OCEAN, APRIL 2018

I was swimming in a small pod of only male dolphins. We were supposed to scan the surrounding area, search for new hunting spots, and look out for regions where predators that threatened our existence swam.

On our way, we saw a docked boat in which a group of humans was hanging out. The leader of our pod led us there and we spent a long time playing around with them, which I didn't particularly enjoy. I never liked humans, since I used to hear horrendous stories about how they treat marine life, so I never comprehended the reason we interacted with them so willingly. Couldn't this group of humans be among the dangerous ones, like the ones who kidnapped some of my mom's friends a long time ago? The story of how they kidnapped them always terrified me to no end.

My mom would always tell me, "We don't hate orcas, even though they kill many of us, because that's how they're destined to feed. Just like we're supposed to feed on sardines, herrings, and so on. That's life, a biological cycle where each species is meant to feed on the one below it, no bad or good guys, just a destiny that needs to be fulfilled. All you can do is try and protect yourself as much as you can, and if you succeed, it's good for you because you get to live a long life. If you fail, it's good for the orcas." Whenever the conversation, however, shifted to humans, she would speak with a different tone, "Humans are the curse we suffer from. A human being is the only creature that steals another creature's life just for entertainment purposes, and even worse, sometimes they just hold us hostage for entertainment as well."

My mother's words echoed in my head as we were playing around the humans' boat. I asked our leader, "What if they want to murder us or take us as hostage?" He jumped in the air, spun his body three times, and caught a large fish that the humans threw at him from the deck, then he let himself dive deep into the water before he floated to the surface once more. He approached me and said, "Humans aren't the same, son." He continued, "Those ones, for instance, are nice. They're here just to have fun, like us! They don't have bad intentions. Do you know how I know? Well, when you turn twenty like me, you will be able to easily distinguish between the evil ones and the good ones. Your ultrasounds will be able to determine the contents of the boat, and you will know if it has dangerous elements in it."

After we left them, he taught me more things about humans, "Poor creatures, they suffer from one of the most difficult conflicts among all living beings, and it's usually the reason behind the cruelty that some of them develop. Ever since they are born, they struggle with themselves! They don't know what they want and they carry the curse of having too many options, most of which they can't even achieve. They have too many aspirations they can't reach, and an endless amount of greed that is imprinted in their cells. They can't get rid of it, as it's part of their nature. Humans suffer a tragic struggle between what they want but can't have, a lot of unreachable dreams, and a craving that carries pain through its repercussions. However, that doesn't mean that they're in hell or that they don't have privileges that make up for all those tragedies." He proceeded to recount things that humans have but we don't and said that even though we're safe from the conflicts they go through, we still can't enjoy many of their blessings. After almost an hour of comparing our lives to theirs, he asked me, "If you had the chance to become human, would you take it?" I thought about it and said, "I simply want to fulfill my destiny, I'm not greedy like them or want what I can't have." He whistled and clicked while moving his tail flukes, then said, laughing, "Do you know that we're the only water creatures that think wisely? In fact, very few dolphins reach that level of wise thinking, a very rare species does... looks like you belong to them, like me!"

He told the rest of the pod to go on their way and asked me, "If there was a place where you could try the human experience with all its privileges and without pain, would you go?" I immediately remembered the old tale and asked, "You mean the magical island?" It was a renowned tale about a magical island where dolphins turned into humans as soon as they touched the shore, then they would transform back into dolphins when they returned to the water. It was said that it's a hidden island that you can't look for; instead, it finds those who are worthy of it.

"I think you are one of the worthy ones, son! You have a pearl of rare wisdom and an interesting brain," he told me. I was full of doubt, "Are you one of the worthy ones too? Did you ever visit it?" He nodded in agreement, so I asked, "What was your experience there like?" He leaped high in the air, dove back to the water, and swam around me, "I can't ever describe the pleasure of stepping on the ground with real feet, where you can feel the sand melt beneath your soles and the gravel surround your skin, or what it feels like to inhale the breeze without water, as your lungs are taken over by the mist of flowers and the fragrance of the grassy hills. I can't describe the pleasure of climbing trees and moving between them while gathering different types of fruits on your way, then biting them with your teeth and slowly savoring their juices. There is the pleasure of grilling fish after adding some delicious flavors and trying out an entirely different taste from the ones we try. There's so much beauty on land, such as grass-covered mountains, water springs, blooming flowers. Even the experience of sleeping on a bed, or the ground even, has a different pleasure than how we sleep. Every sense they have has its own pleasure, and only humans have that. Their biggest tragedy is that they're too used to those privileges, that they no longer understand their values, and here comes an advantage that we have. We, the dolphins worthy of the island, never get bored of those pleasures, simply because they are not lasting for us. We only experience the island for a couple of days, then we head back to the water."

He informed me that the group of humans we'd seen on the boat worked hard and saved money to spend a couple of days by the ocean and enjoy watching us. "That same ocean that we're so used to living in that it became an ordinary thing for us! Visiting the island and roaming around in it as a human, is a fun yet free trip!" I wondered how he knew all that information about humans, so he answered, "The island, son! It provides you with a large amount of knowledge on humans, their lives, their habits, and their languages. Did you know that every group of people have their own language? I know that, and I even know how to speak their language when I'm human, even though no human can visit that island."

My desire to visit the island overwhelmed me, so I asked him how to get there. "The first rule is that you shouldn't speak about it, not to your mother, your friends, or your girlfriend. The second rule is that you have to be enduring. The road to the island is risky and troublesome, and you have to pass by an area filled with orcas before you get there. You have to escape them, then you have to spend two days swimming in the arid ocean, that part which is devoid of any fish, guidance, or land. Once you pass the most terrifying part of the ocean, then the island will find you."

ARWA—VENICE, JUNE 2018

I didn't like Paris! I think the main reason behind that is that I always pictured this enchanting city of lights whenever I dreamt about visiting it. Before we traveled, Kamel asked me which cities I desired to visit, and of course, I picked Paris. I didn't picture it, however, to be so crowded, with long lines everywhere you go. You spend three hours standing in a line under the Eiffel tower so you could stay there for only one hour. Kamel, who was passionate about museums, made us spend a whole day at the Louvre, where most of the day was wasted on the suffocating lines.

The most beautiful time we spent there was at the Palace of Versailles, which we entered through a golden gate, after standing in a very long line of course. We entered the Hall of Mirrors, which had large gilded mirrors and gilded gates. I have no idea how they acquired this amount of gold! As much as I was impressed with the intricacy of architecture, the gardens were a different story. They resembled paintings of trees, grass, ponds, and sculptures; I thought they were even more remarkable than the paintings that filled the Louvre. The captivating night performance in the garden reminded me of the operettas I watched in old black-and-white movies, but I was too exhausted to enjoy it.

I envied Marie Antoinette when I saw where she resided: a smaller palace which was constructed a short distance from the grand one. I didn't envy her for the life she had in that palace or for the extremely beautiful furniture. What I envied her for was that she didn't have to go through those large crowds to witness that beauty. Crowdedness really does ruin anything beautiful. If I had the chance to walk in that palace, just me and Kamel, it would have been even more fascinating than our first night together.

I apologize for that exaggerative metaphor since our actual first night together erased all the bad memories about men in history. We spent it in a hotel by the Nile, which added a new taste to the Nile that night that I have never experienced in my entire life. That night, Kamel was a prince and I his princess, then he became a flirtatious young boy and I was his playful girl, and eventually, he became the only man in the world and I the only woman. Kamel inaugurated my femininity on that night in a way that made me explore sensations I didn't know I had. At that moment, I think I beat Marie Antoinette. If she owned a palace that she didn't have to share with thousands of visitors, I had a man who made me discover a new world more magical than all palaces combined. Moreover, no women shared him with me like women jostled to get her men, be it her husband or lover.

Before we traveled to Paris, he went to Dubai to see his children and spent five days there, during which I deeply longed for him to come back, especially after I had tasted heaven in his arms. We spoke every night, during which he expressed his yearning for me, while I described to him how much I missed his touches that I had become addicted to. We met each other in Dubai's airport, which was my transit for my plane to Paris, and due to how much we missed each other, he paid for a hotel room in the airport's hotel. We spent a couple of hours there before heading to Paris, which received me coldly with its long, crowded lines in the Charles De Gaulle Airport.

Venice was different. We didn't plan to go there at first, but Kamel felt like something was missing. I think the reason he felt that way was that he didn't see the beam in my eyes that he saw on the night he took me out for dinner in Al-Suhaymi's House, and he was right. Usually, our fascination with things stems from our expectations or the picture we painted in our heads for that thing. I wasn't expecting what I saw in Al-Suhaymi's house. Actually, I expected a dull and long night. Instead, I was surprised by everything that the stranger, at the time, had planned for me. On the contrary, I had high expectations for Paris, the first foreign city I visited with my husband. To be honest, Kamel did try his best to make me happy, but the crowdedness only made me want to get back to our hotel room as soon as we could.

Venice welcomed us without any crowding in the airport, but the city itself was crowded. In Paris, Kamel knew what he was doing, as he took me by the hand and guided me. In Venice, he was exploring the place and lost his way there just like I did, which gave me the impression that Venice was our first place together. In Paris, I felt like the ghost of another woman, or several others, which was another heavy feeling I carried there with me that made me enjoy the city even less.

The crowdedness in Venice reminded me of the one in Downtown Cairo during the Eid[14] Season, the one you have fun breaking into as you take on the challenge (unlike the dull, long lines in Paris). We went on a gondola ride, which is the most famous activity in Venice, where the captain offered us a free trip. I immediately accepted it, thanking him, but Kamel laughed and said in English, "Nothing is for free, especially here in Italy!" but the man swore that we weren't going to pay a penny.

The ride was destined to end up on Murano Island. I quickly went on google to look it up and discovered that it was famous for glass-making. The pictures available on the internet depicted many glass sculptures and fascinating masterpieces, but nothing exceeded the beauty of the island itself and the houses on it, which is what made me insist to go on a trip, despite Kamel's doubts.

It was supposed to go off at four, and it was still two at the time, so we went to the hotel to have lunch. On our way back to the port, we passed by St. Mark's square, in front of a church we intended to visit the following day. I saw a group of men, each wearing a large black cap that covered a dark-blue suit and a tie. Their outfits reminded me of some movie I couldn't remember, but it had a look

[14] A religious holiday celebrated by Muslims

that indicated mystery and adventure. I asked Kamel to ask them what they did, to which Kamel laughed and said they simply worked at the fancy café and that their costume was meant to attract crazy foreigners like the two of us, who visited a café to drink a cup of coffee five times more expensive than it's supposed to be. I shook my head, grabbed him by the hand, and said, "Then let's head to our free trip."

When we arrived on Murano island, I understood why the trip was free. They didn't let us enjoy the beauty of the island, but they took us to a desolate side of it that looked upon a factory's glass door. When we spotted the name written on the sign, Kamel gasped and asked me to re-check the name carefully. I didn't understand what he meant, so he reiterated, "Stephan Rosti[15]! Don't you know who that is? The actor with the famous cinema line?" I frowned in confusion, so he imitated a familiar voice that I recognized from old black and white movies, but I never knew the actor's name. I looked again at the sign, then looked at Kamel with a smile and said jokingly, "Maybe his kids built a factory here and put his name on the signboard?"

They led us to a large workshop where a man was performing glassblowing. He was restructuring it into a professionally made horse shape with intermingling blue and red colors. He was quite skilled at what he was doing, but I didn't enjoy the show, so the tour guide gave me the horse to regain my attention. Kamel printed a kiss on my

---

[15] (16 November 1891—22 May 1964) An Egyptian film actor and director, his mother was Egyptian-Italian

cheek, as he seemingly enjoyed the childlike happiness that sparkled in my eyes when I was given the horse.

They then took us on a tour of the glass museum in the upper level of the workshop, which I understood to be the main reason for the trip. The pieces in the workshop there looked like antiquities found in museums. I heard a British lady, who was a part of our group, asking about the price of a glass-bird statue, and in no time, I heard her gasp in disapproval from how overly expensive the piece was. I laughed and told Kamel, "You can't fool women easily, even foreigners!" to which he said with a laugh, "They fooled you and brought you here, didn't they?" I pinched his arms lightheartedly, then pulled him by the hand to watch the rest of the exhibits.

On our way back, the British lady was still cursing the factory and its workers, accusing them of roguery and overpricing their items. Kamel and I were holding in our laughs throughout her protests and until we finally went back. There, he asked me to have coffee at that fancy café we saw earlier, but I said no and suggested walking around instead. The streets were all very narrow, mostly tiny alleys that branched out and split, but they were all clean and organized. They had lines of different shops, like gift shops and antiquities shops, as well as restaurants and cafes that looked much more affordable than the ones in the square. We sat in one of those cafes, and I was surprised to see Kamel open up a leather bag and get the glass jewelry set that I saw and liked in Murano. I didn't remember seeing him buy it, so I exclaimed in dazzlement and asked him for its price, but he ignored my question. Instead, he asked me to put it on for him when we got back to the hotel. I couldn't control myself and kissed him on lips, then I looked around nervously like a naughty student who just made a mistake. He smiled, took my hand, and printed a long kiss on it that lasted until the waiter came with our coffee.

ARWA—CAIRO, AUGUST 2018

Tuesday was the day of my appointment with Nehad, my gynecologist and good friend. I paid her a visit with Kamel earlier when we first got married after he suggested that I insert an IUD. On that day, Nehad reassured me in her typical humorous manner, informing me that women in their thirties like she and I always found this method to be the easiest and safest. In that more recent visit, however, I went alone because I wanted to check on some abdominal cramps that attacked me every now and then.

I sat in the waiting room of her clinic, a big reception area with a large screen that played videos on women's health issues and showed Dr. Nehad's skills in handling them. It was a luxurious clinic that her husband had furnished and then given to her as a present after she earned her master's degree. Their marriage was a source of envy among many, but I was one of the very few people who knew the reality behind it. For example, I knew how much she suffered from many issues she never expressed and how she invested herself in her career so she could spend as much time as possible away from her husband.

I asked the secretary to admit me when it was my turn without informing Nehad that I was waiting in the clinic so it wouldn't cause any inconvenience for her. I opened my phone, the one that Kamel bought me on his last visit to Dubai, as I suddenly felt a rush of nostalgia about our second day in Venice. I stared at one of the pictures, showing Kamel while he was debating with our tour guide. She was recounting the history of St. Mark's Basilica and talking about the human remains that were transported from Alexandria to Venice, while Kamel insisted that those remains belonged to Egypt and had to be brought back to their home country. We were standing in front of a shrine where photography was restricted, but he looked so attractive at that moment that it made me sneakily get out my phone and take a secret picture.

I swiped to another picture of the two of us together inside Doge's Palace[16] standing in front of a painting the size of a wall. In the picture, he was whispering sweet nothings in my ears while I blushed at his words. I contemplated another picture where we stood in front of some ancient shields, while Kamel jokingly suggested I put one on and I giggled at his suggestion. The last picture I swiped to was a picture of the palace's prison wall, which had several writings on it. I remember how we spent a long time trying to decipher the meanings behind them; I insisted they were love letters, whereas Kamel

[16] One of the main landmarks of the city of Venice in northern Italy. It used to be the residence of the Doge of Venice, the supreme authority of the former Republic

assumed that they were written complaints against the cruelty and oppression of prison. Those memories were my source of strength during the times when he was away from me, visiting his kids in Dubai.

The secretary interrupted my thoughts when she told me it was my turn. Nehad's welcome was, as usual, quite warm. She suggested checking up on me first, then we could chitchat for a while. After everything turned out normal in my checkup, she simply prescribed a painkiller and some topical medications. She then sat with me on the couch and asked about Kamel, to which I responded that he was still in Dubai.

"I can't begin to imagine how tricky your situation is, but then again, no relationship is clear of trouble," she said. "I want you to be clever and whine about your marriage in front of your friends from time to time. Don't show off your happiness too much, especially in front of Naglaa, she's a jinx." I laughed at her remark, but she asked me again to be extra cautious. Nehad was never the type of person who feared envy or who obsessed over people's words, but ever since things got drastically worse between her and her husband, she started to believe that there was a hidden, secret reason behind their issues. She believed that people, no matter how much they care for you, couldn't help but envy a happy woman, because the mere presence of a happy woman is a rare occasion.

I wanted to stay longer with her, but I figured that her patients were probably getting bored waiting for their turns, so I left her after promising to visit again soon. As soon as I got into my car, I opened my phone to text Kamel, but I found a notification of a message that was sent by a stranger. The message read, "I'm in Cairo, can we meet?" I soon realized it was sent by Kamel's ex-wife when I noticed her Facebook name, "Dorreya Al-Iraqy." Of course, I had looked her up a couple of times out of curiosity, but I never imagined she would want to meet me.

I considered telling Kamel, but I froze. I lost my capacity to think or make a decision. I contemplated her profile picture like I was seeing her for the first time. She was posing with her two sons as they all wore skiwear in a closed area, which could have been either Ski Dubai or Ski Egypt[17]. Her facial features weren't that clear in the picture, so I couldn't determine her level of physical beauty. In addition, the skiwear concealed the details of her physique, so I didn't know whether she was fitter or fuller than me.

"OK, we can meet now if you are available," I texted her back. I thought it was a good opportunity, despite its distressing possibilities. Her message meant she knew exactly who I was and knew about my marriage to Kamel. He didn't, however, tell me she knew! How could he hide something like that from me? Was it possible that they agreed to get back together, but she insisted that he let her meet me first? If that was the case, he would have given her my phone number. My thoughts were interrupted by her message, in which she agreed to meet me and suggested to meet at Cilantro, the location close to my office.

---

[17] Indoor Ski Resorts in the cities of Dubai and Cairo, respectively

I arrived and found her waiting for me. At first glance, her clothes appeared pretty normal, but after a closer look, I realized that her outfit included more high-end fashion brands than I could count. Her jacket was embroidered with the Chanel logo, and underneath it, she wore an elegant shirt but I couldn't recognize its brand. It was ornamented, however, with a Swarovski necklace which I recognized from its famous swan logo. It was a gold necklace with shiny stones all over it. Her wristwatch was Dior, and her purse, which she put on the table in front of me, was Armani. Oh, I almost forgot to mention that she was an attractive lady with hazel eyes and clear skin that wasn't painted with too much makeup. She had full, carefully lined lips. During those first moments, she was also checking me out, and I believe she made a series of assumptions about me in the first couple of seconds that we met.

The waitress came to our table and we both ordered juices, which she insisted she would pay for. "I'm the one who asked to meet you!" She then added, laughing, "Plus, I'm the older one here!" I nodded and smiled politely. She began to introduce herself, saying that she married Kamel around fifteen years ago, traveled to Dubai with him, and worked at a reputable real estate company there. After that, she was able to found her own company with an Emirati friend of hers, and her career had been flourishing ever since. The way she talked reminded me of a person who was narrating their work experience at an interview, which I didn't understand. She noticed I was getting impatient, so she said, "Let's get to the point! I'm completely fine with your marriage to Kamel, even though I still haven't told him I know about it yet. But I did want to meet you and introduce myself to you to remove any negative picture that Kamel might've made up about me since I'm used to him being a pathological liar."

That was the beginning of her attack on Kamel, but she rapidly moved past that point and stated that she wanted to guarantee we had a good relationship with each other in case my marriage to Kamel continued and we had children together, as she wanted my future children and hers to be a source of support to each other instead of becoming enemies. Her story with Kamel—according to her version—revolved around her being a loyal wife and him being an unfaithful man who couldn't stop himself from getting into one relationship after the other, in addition to some additional questionable, paid encounters. I felt a lump in my throat, as I tried to convince myself that everything she was saying was gibberish and that Kamel's romantic adventures only started after their divorce, but she said, "I'm sure he convinced you that those relationships began after our divorce, but in reality, they were the reason behind it." She proceeded to claim that she endured everything for the sake of their children and that she caught him with other women countless times, after which he would sob like a child and swear it was never going to happen again.

"After one of his adventures, during which he got a second wife; a much younger woman whom he later divorced, I forced him to write half of his possessions under our children's names in the form of real estate that my company managed."

She claimed that she did it to guarantee that her children's rights were reserved since Kamel was extremely generous with his women with both his money and emotions. He would shower them with excessive romantic words, gifts, and trips to make them believe they were the only ones in his life. "I gave up on him as a husband and partner two years before our divorce. I only stayed with him for the kids, but I eventually couldn't take it anymore after he transmitted a disease that he contracted from one of the whores he used to know."

The information I received kept accumulating and formed a fatal flood in my heart. Even if she was somewhat exaggerating her story, there must have been some truth in it. First of all, she behaved and looked like a rational lady and a successful businesswoman, opposite to how Kamel described her to me. In addition, her reason for taking over his money was more reasonable than his questionable justification. I excused myself to go to the bathroom, where I stood alone to plan my reaction. I didn't want to react impulsively, especially since Dorreya had prepared every word beforehand without depicting the true intentions behind them. Was it possible that she still loved him and simply wanted to end our marriage to get him back? Or did she want to take revenge and destroy his happiness? Did she genuinely want to warn me and reveal his truth to me? If it was the last option, then she was some sort of saint who flew all the way from Dubai to rescue me from Kamel's hell.

I returned and sat with her once more. She was about to continue talking when I interrupted her, "This still doesn't justify why you wanted to meet me!" She smiled, staring into my eyes, and said, "Why do you think?" to which I responded coldly, "I don't like to guess. If you're done, please allow me to excuse myself." She stopped me before I could do it and proceeded to talk calmly, assuring me that the main reason was the interest of her children. "Kamel has plenty of money and real estate, I don't want him to keep wasting them on meaningless adventures. Trust me, I wish your marriage could last so it controls his behavior somehow or stop him from wasting his money. I want him to save it for my children, and potentially yours."

I expected her to ask me to not tell him about our encounter, but surprisingly, she asked me to confront him about it and test his loyalty to me by asking him to announce our marriage and try for kids. I told her, "Who told you we're not planning to have kids?" She smirked and said, "It's the same story over and over, they all have the same tricks and tales, starting from the half-open mouth hand kiss. Listen, you look like a decent lady, maybe the first one I could trust from Kamel's women. I wouldn't mind your kids to become my children's siblings, at least it's better than him getting with a foreigner who gives him a child that isn't even his." She concluded the last part of her argument like a lawyer who was done with her pleading in front of the judges in court.

It was a lot to take in! Kamel's story was filled with drama, during both the good and bad parts. I said, "What if you just want him to get back to you?" She let out a sardonic laugh and said, "Kamel is out of my life for good. He has enough energy and passion for women that will prevent him from staying faithful to one woman only. Plus, I have my own plans. I'm a woman and I have needs too." She got up, extended her hand to shake mine, wished me luck, and apologized if my words hurt me. "But that's life, you simply have to accept it."

ZIAD—SOUTH PACIFIC OCEAN, MAY 2018

The time still hadn't come for me to go to the magical island yet, at least that's what the old dolphin told me. He didn't give me a reason or set a specific time, but he mentioned it was meant to be soon without elaborating any further. As I slept, the alert half of my brain would contemplate the trip more than it would be concerned with watching for potential predators or picking times to rise to the water's surface and breathe. As for the sleeping half of my brain, it would get drawn to mysterious dreams about the island and the pleasures of using feet, climbing hills, and picking fresh fruits.

Maya, another friend of ours called Nader, and I decided to go hunting in a new area that Nader, who is one year older than me, had suggested. He claimed that his mother took him hunting in that midwater area plenty of times. It was close to the barrier reef, where plenty of fish hid beneath its soft ocean floor. We swam to the bottom with our bodies close to each other while playing around and nudging one another lightly with our fins. We descended in a vertical direction until we finally reached the bottom, where the water was muddy and the vision poor. We began to blame Nader for his suggestion, which initially seemed stupid, but he disregarded our protests and approached a certain spot in the sand with his rostrum. He aggressively stuck it in there, caught a hiding fish, and devoured it whole.

We followed his lead and began to search for fish underneath the seabed, but to no avail. Nader himself didn't get lucky again. He turned around, faced us, and said "Now, we wait!" I clicked bitterly, "For what?" He let out a whistle while pointing in the direction of two stingray fish, claiming they were outfitted with electrical sensors that made them sense the natural electrical charges of potential prey in hiding, so all we had to do was wait, watch them and share the food they found. However, we still had to be careful not to go near their tails, which can sting painfully. His idea turned out to be successful, as we were eventually able to maintain plentiful food. Nader was prancing all over the place to celebrate the success of his idea as if he came up with a ground-breaking scientific discovery. If only I could inform him I was among a very rare species that had the privilege to go to a magical island where dolphins were transformed into humans! He would be green with envy, but I had to follow the old dolphin's instructions and keep my snout shut.

While were still occupied with swimming, fooling around, and having fun, in addition to joyously celebrating our adventure, we were taken aback when we spotted a large pod of strange-looking all-male dolphins. They were heading towards us with great speed as the noises they emitted depicted animosity and violence. In that kind of situation, we would normally try to escape and send out distress calls to our pod so they would come along and rescue us. However, we were quickly surrounded by that strange pod, which didn't give us a chance to escape. We desperately tried to avoid their attacks, but we were soon scratched and hurt by them, especially since we failed at trying to escape and our distress calls got lost. Our calls were barely able to get out among their loud and overpowering noises. The three of us became closely attached, but I paid more attention to trying to protect Maya so I could keep her from getting hurt as much as I could.

Eventually, they seemed to get bored of their little game, as they suddenly stopped attacking but remained surrounding us anyway. I finally found a gap in their circle from which Maya and I were able to escape, while Nader followed our lead. They chased us for a short amount of time until they stopped when they realized we were getting deeper into the bottom area of the barrier reef. We were nearly running out of breath, so we had to try and swim to the surface to catch some air. However, we got lost amid coral reefs that surrounded us from all directions.

Maya started to panic when she noticed a tortoise's skeleton. She was convinced that it was lost in the deep sea like her until it ran out of breath and choked to death. Nader initially made fun of her, but he started to get into a panic attack himself when he spotted the skeleton of a small dolphin that also appeared to choke to death. I gathered my strength and ordered them to follow me and quit panicking. I produced a long noise until I was finally able to find an opening through the coral reefs, so I quickly headed towards it. There, I noticed some sunlight passing through, so I went through the opening while whistling happily, followed by Maya and Nader.

Our jumps in the air were so high as we were joyous with success. Luckily, a large wave came our way and propelled the three of us along, raising us as we took in oxygen and filled our longing lungs with fresh air. We repeated our jumps while trying to keep up with the large waves as the top of our heads could barely rise above them. We would then let ourselves dive into them once more. During that time, I noticed that Maya and Nader were getting closer than usual, which gave me the impression that they were about to form a couple of some sort.

I always considered Maya a friend, just like I did Nader. I never thought of her as a partner or a mother to my future calves, except on very rare occasions. For instance, when the old dolphin first told me about the magical island, I considered whether Maya was one of the chosen dolphins as well. I decided not to get any closer to her until I found out, as I told myself, "If I'm one of the rare species, then I must choose a female who's just like me." I was completely prepared for that female to be any other dolphin that isn't Maya. Despite that, I still felt some sort of unease when I noticed she was getting closer to Nader, even though I was sure that the reason behind that was that I stepped back and created a distance between us.

The three of us felt physically exhausted because of the wounds we had. We all felt the need to treat them, so I suggested we swim to the bottom of the water in a nearby area where we could find gorgonians that aid with the healing of wounds, scratches, and especially bites of aggressive dolphins and other marine creatures. Maya agreed to my suggestion while Nader hesitated, mentioning that we had to return since we had left our pod a long time ago. He eventually, however, gave in to my suggestion.

We dove into an area of my choice, where softly dancing gorgonians awaited us at the bottom. Their branches extended like the feathers of a large, colorful bird. Both Maya and Nader froze, then proceeded to swim in their places, as they didn't know how to utilize the corals to heal themselves. I swam proudly in front of them, rubbing my wounds and scratches against the soft, loose corals while moving back and forth in a calm dance-like motion that I called "the healing dance." Maya decided to end her reluctance and imitated me, joining me in my healing dance. Nader later followed until we all felt our wounds were healed, then we decided to swim to the surface once more.

We ran into another obstacle on our way to the surface, as we found a pod of orcas nearby. Since we were only three, it would be easy for them to eat us once they noticed us. I quickly stepped into the role of the leader and began to explain our escape plan, "We're faster than orcas but they can breathe for longer periods, so we have to rely on distracting them, then…" I was interrupted by

Maya before continuing to explain my full plan, as she asked me to stay quiet and listen.

Initially, I didn't understand what she meant, but I listened to her and stayed quiet. I began to hear a deep sound, like a long call that was emitted with a sorrowful pitch. It turned out to be the sound of a female humpback whale sending out a distress call. We sighed in relief as we realized what was going on: the orcas weren't interested in us, they wanted to hunt an entire delicious, filling humpback baby whale that would be sufficient for them to share. We swam away until we reached a safe distance, then we continued watching.

We noticed the orcas swimming in circles around the female whale to create a powerful whirlpool that would overwhelm her so it could become an easier task for them to steal her baby. The female whale emitted another distress alarm while still trying to protect it. She finally received a response from a nearby area, as a male whale announced he was on his way to defend her and the little one. I told May and Nader assertively, "I hope you enjoyed watching that mini-show, but if the male whale gets here and defends the baby, they won't have any other option but to eat us." Nader agreed with me, but Maya begged, "I want to make sure the baby whale's fine. I swam with him a couple of days ago." Nader protested, saying, "If we stay here to make sure he's fine, who's going to make sure that we are?" I let out a laughing whistle and dove deep into the water, heading towards the direction of our pod while they both followed me. Maya, however, remained mad at us.

ARWA—PORTO, PORTUGAL—SEPTEMBER 2018

Kamel only changed after he met me, that was the fact that he confirmed the first time we saw each other after my monumental encounter with Dorreya, his ex-wife. Today, on a beach on the Atlantic Ocean in Porto, Portugal, I felt the genuineness of this "fact" he said earlier. We were watching the high ocean waves from afar; the size of one wave was easily double the size of any wave I ever saw on the North Coast here in Egypt.

Kamel admitted to everything Dorreya had said about him, but he insisted that all those adventures were in the past. He emphasized his deep love for me and how I was the only exception (which was an exaggeration I openly welcomed). When he was explaining the extent of his love for me and how much it had changed him, he wasn't sobbing. Even though his eyes welled up and the tears fought to roll down his cheeks, he tried to suppress them as much as he could. If he had wailed that time, I wouldn't have believed him as much, because it's easy for anyone to pretend they're crying, but it's almost impossible to pretend that they're preventing themselves from crying.

At that moment, he appeared to be more offended and vulnerable rather than in pain. It felt like if he let himself cry, it would deeply hurt his pride. He insisted that he never transmitted an STD to his wife and that she only assumed he did because her gynecologist told her there was a small chance the disease she had could be sexually transmitted yet the bigger probability happens due to natural causes. She, however, resorted to the former justification, since she wanted a divorce and finally found her strong motive. When I confronted him about lying about the romantic adventures only happening after his divorce, he apologized and claimed that he was scared I'd leave him if he had told me the truth.

That night, I didn't let him come near me or fulfill any of his desires, ignoring my own fiery desires as well. I asked him to leave me alone so I could think properly. I convinced myself that Dorreya did what she did because she still had feelings for Kamel and despised seeing a new woman in his life, especially one that threatened her in every way. After all, I wasn't a fling or some casual affair. I thought to myself, "Maybe I can change him, make him loyal. After all, I'm beautiful, successful, smart, and strong. I'm an elegant lady at times and a playful temptress at other times, which is the combination that makes any man disregard his desires for other women. Maybe Dorreya truly wanted to warn me, maybe she saw a good stepmother to her children in me, but deep down, there must be unspoken intentions." In English, Kamel said, "It just doesn't make sense!" referring to her reasons for wanting to meet me. I understood where he was coming from; that woman was either still in love with him or wanted to deny him any happiness outside of their life together.

It all worked out for the best, anyway. Our encounter was some sort of blessing in disguise because, throughout the following couple of days, we finally began to announce our marriage in our workplace. We had a reception in one of those banquet halls that held weddings and events. We lived together in his main apartment, where we welcomed plenty of guests that wanted to congratulate us, many of whom were friends of mine who were visiting with their husbands. We went to the sporting club together many times and walked around hand-in-hand in front of people. It was a big change that made up for the stressful days that followed my meeting with Dorreya. Despite everything, something inside me still felt anxious, which led me to tell him I didn't want to try for kids for another year. He didn't object to my suggestion. He came into my office one day and told me to apply for a vacation request because we were going on a ten-day trip. His program included two days in Dubai, three days in Brussels, and three days in Porto, Portugal. The purpose behind visiting Dubai was to meet his kids and spend a long day with them. After that, he had a conference to attend in Brussels, and lastly, the reason for heading to Porto was a surprise that he insisted on keeping to himself.

All women care about having three desires fulfilled by men: romantic desires, physical desires, and shopping desires. Before going on that trip, Kamel had already fulfilled the first two, but after we spent two days in Dubai, he satisfied my last desire like never before. In the Dubai Mall[18], I shopped in ten shops, most of which were high-end fashion brands that I always dreamed about buying from. I saw the Dubai Fountain[19] and the breathtaking Burj Khalifa[20]. Kamel didn't think it was enough for me to watch the fountain from the common, crowded area, so he took me to a Lebanese restaurant that had a terrace that offered a direct view of the fountain. He chose for us to go at exactly 10 a.m., when the fountain's water formed waves to the song "Enta Omry[21]." The tunes of the music mixed with the pumping of the fountain and the soft trickling of its water, in addition to the voice of Kamel, who was humming the song with me. His radiant face, tender smile, and loving eyes mixed with the water's tranquil dance and fascinating lights that went up for meters along with the water, looking like attractive dancing flames.

We spent the following day with Kamel's two kids: Anas, a fourteen-year-old, and Bahaa, a ten-year-old; they were two well-mannered kids that were way more fluent

---

[18] A shopping mall in Dubai, and the second largest mall in the world

[19] The world's tallest performing fountain, situated in the city of Dubai

[20] A skyscraper, famous landmark and the tallest tower in the world

[21] In English: "You Are My Life," a popular Egyptian song by Umm Khulthum

in speaking English than Arabic. They welcomed me and were being excessively nice like I was an old friend or a relative. I was thankful they were boys and not girls, because the case might have been different in the latter situation, and our meeting might have been more stressful with ulterior motives. On that day, I went shopping again. Of course, I didn't buy as many things as the day before, but it was still more than a whole month worth of shopping.

Brussels had a green welcome in store for me. Our plane landed in an airport far away from the city, then a car drove us there. We passed by large green fields that erased the image of the luxurious buildings that impressed me in Dubai. On our first day, he took me shopping again, as he seemed to be well aware how important shopping is to women. On the next day, we attended his conference, where he introduced me to some of his foreign and Arab peers. We had dinner with them in a light, cheery atmosphere, one that was distinctly different from the work events we had in Egypt. The most beautiful thing I saw in Brussels was a garden we saw from the terrace of a restaurant where we had lunch. Most of its space was filled with groups of bushes, trees, and flowers that appeared like a carefully embroidered carpet from above. When I shared that image with Kamel, he explained that they do compare it to a carpet indeed. The waitress, an olive-skinned woman with a flirtatious smile, came and asked us where we were from. She spoke in English but had a French accent. Before Kamel could respond, I immediately said, "We're from Egypt!" She proceeded to converse with us, telling us about her Arabic origins and how much she adored Egypt and wished to visit it someday. I interrupted her talkativeness and asked her to bring us the menu, but I was unfortunately forced to let Kamel communicate with her because the names of the dishes were confusing to me. The waitress walked away gracefully, swiveling her hips, while I watched her bitterly as I muttered to myself. Kamel laughed at me, which in return made me angrier and almost made me get in a fight with him, but he kissed me on the lips to keep me quiet.

Another waiter arrived, a middle-aged man in a formal suit and a tie, while a younger waiter stood behind him. He was dragging a serving cart that had small plates that surrounded a large plate covered by a stainless-steel dome cover. The young waiter placed the small plates, which had different types of salads, in front of us, before revealing the last plate, which had a large baguette on it. The man got out a fork and a knife and skillfully separated the baguette into two halves, then laid them on their sides, which in return revealed a whole seabass fish underneath it. He proceeded to cut the fish into tiny pieces with a different set of cutlery, then he would put those pieces in front of us, while I watched his precision in astonishment. He didn't leave our table until the large plate only had the skeleton of the fish, whereas the meaty parts were on our plates. He was doing his job so skillfully that it felt like he'd been doing it all his life.

That night in our hotel room, I asked him why he smiled when I was watching that waiter in the restaurant. "You treat me like a kid that you're dragging along to the amusement park," I told him. He laughed at my analogy and said, "I smile because I love you! I love all your details, your reaction, every muscle that moves on your face makes my heart flutter." I responded, "Do you know that I also love watching your expressions, especially when..." I stopped my sentence and smiled bashfully. He boldly gazed at me and said, "Are we just going to keep on talking or do you want to remember those expressions together?" I lightly clapped him on the shoulder with my hand, which he grabbed then kissed on both sides, depicting his submission to his queen, me. He began to gradually climb up the monarchial ladder until he settled in his natural place, where he became my king and I submitted to his control. He proceeded to play around with me in whichever way he pleased, moving me around, listening to me, taking from me, and giving me. He then readjusted my face towards the direction of the mirror so I could enjoy watching both his expressions and mine; all new feelings I knew nothing about before my marriage to Kamel, that man who made me feel both holiness and nudity at the same time.

We flew to Porto in a small plane that greatly resembled a bus. We stayed in a hotel that overlooked the Douro River, near its river-mouth in the ocean. Porto was my favorite city; it was a quiet city with loving residents, effortless beauty, and bearable crowdedness. I never felt like a stranger there. The corniche was pleasant, and the aerial tramway showed off the beauty of the city. I fell in love with the streets paved with cobblestone, similar to the ones in old Cairo, the large river-mouth which smoothly mixed with ocean water, and even its beaches that were unfortunately closed due to high waves.

Kamel took me to a different part of the city: a tower that had a distinct feel from where we were staying. We sat somewhere inside it, where Kamel introduced me to a real estate consultant. He informed me that he was helping him buy a place to potentially reside there in Porto, which would later allow us to obtain the residency in Portugal. The man proceeded to explain the system in Portugal and the advantages of different real estate in Porto, before eventually thanking us and excusing himself. "What's hindering me is lack of finance," Kamel told me. "I'm waiting for a chance to convince Dorreya to put the money she saved under the kids' name here under real state in my name instead. At first, I was hesitant to take that step of buying something in this city, but now that I see how much you love it, I will find a way to buy a property no matter what. Porto will be our main sanctuary in the future."

ARWA—CAIRO, JANUARY 2019

My days with Kamel went on peacefully; they were only disturbed by that occasional week he spent in Dubai from time to time. During that week, my uncertainties would affect me as I wondered how he was spending his time there. Doubts invaded my heart like a snake that hisses before it strikes. Sometimes I pondered the idea of him getting back together with Dorreya, even though it was an unlikely possibility. I mainly, however, wondered if he would get tempted by an attractive, enticing woman that submitted to him with words or action.

Whenever he went away, I began to act like an insecure teenager. I called him almost every other hour and sometimes demanded him to send a picture of himself with the kids. Other times, he would tell me he wanted to go to bed early and then he would turn off his phone, which was enough to drive me crazy and set my jealousy on fire. I eventually asked him to never turn it off under any circumstances. I even suggested that he bring his children to Egypt from time to time instead of traveling to them every time, but he claimed that they were too attached to their lives in Dubai and could no longer be accustomed to life in Egypt.

My mom suddenly became sick with gallstones and her doctor decided she needed an operation. That was during a time when Kamel was in Dubai, so I immediately called him and he showed up the following day, which showed a strong sense of reliability and support. He wanted to pay for the hospital bills, but my father insisted that he had to do it himself. I stayed with my mother for a whole week at the hospital, while tubes entered in and out of her abdomen. I accompanied her all day long, while Kamel would spend most of the day with us, then he would have dinner with me at a restaurant near the hospital, and eventually go to sleep in our house while I slept next to my mom.

I was so deeply moved by his reliability during that period, that it made me stop doubting his intentions and genuinely consider removing my birth control method. I thought he was the right kind of person who I wanted as a father to my future kids; he provided me with love and safety, and never denied me anything I wished for. Of course, that period wasn't the only reason behind my decision, but it helped banish the remaining worries I had about our relationship; he managed to remove many other doubts with his love and generosity.

I intended to share my decision with him after his trip to Dubai, but something disquieting happened when he was there: Hours and hours passed before Kamel would respond to my calls. One time, I decided to send a message to one of his kids to check up on him, but his kid informed me that he hadn't seen him in a month. When Kamel returned, I didn't confront him about it, but I waited until he went to sleep to take a look at his passport and make sure he truly was in Dubai. I did indeed find the entry and exit stamp in and out of Dubai, but what surprised me was that he went on a trip to Azerbaijan without informing me.

I confronted him the following day, to which he said, "I wanted to tell you about it as soon as I woke up, I promise. I went with two of my friends because I wanted to visit Baku, I heard it's a beautiful city with beaches that have many fishing spots, I've always told you how much I enjoy fishing." He justified hiding it from me by claiming that he had promised to take me with him wherever he traveled and that it was the first time that he traveled without me since we got married. He said he wanted to tell me about it after he came back instead of telling me on the phone.

There wasn't much logic behind his explanation, but once again, I tried to take in his argument. I warned him, however, that if he lied to me again, he was going to lose all his credibility. The following day at the office, I was going over some unresolved work issues when I heard one WhatsApp notification sound after the other, which made me leave what I was doing and open my phone. I found several pictures, sent by Kamel, of islands and beautiful landscapes. There were pictures of forests where people swung on ropes hung between trees, coral reefs in deep sees, colorful fishes, whales, and dolphins. There were also pictures of caves which revealed beautiful beaches with palm trees behind them in addition to a large mountain covered in grass and many other breath-taking scenes that made me wish I could somehow get inside those pictures and lose myself in that wondrous paradise.

Kamel followed those pictures by a long text, "As a humble apology from me, feel free to book a trip for the two of us there and plan it however you like." "But I don't know where that place is". "In Tahiti and Bora Bora, two islands in the South Pacific," he said and then sent a link in Arabic that explained everything about both islands, and asked me to book everything, our flight, the hotel, the trips, all within an open budget, to be paid for with the American credit card he gave me a while earlier.

When we went back to our house, I told him it was unnecessary to waste all that money, "What's done is done, and I forgive you, but no trip is going to pay for your mistake no matter how expensive it is." He insisted that he was planning to surprise me either way, but his true apology was in how he was going to let me plan it the way I preferred. He had already taught me how to use the app that plans trips, and how to differentiate between good trips from cheap ones, so he asked me to use it, and I did. Throughout the following days, I was able to plan everything, including the flight from Tahiti to Bora Bora, the accommodation, and the activities. The total budget was extremely high of course, but I went for it so that the money cost of his previous lie was extreme as well. That was the first time I thought in that way about his actions.

One month after this incident, I went for my appointment with Nehad, my friend and gynecologist.

I had been experiencing a couple of odd symptoms, so I wanted to visit her. I asked her to book the last slot for me so we could have dinner together, to which she agreed. I wanted to open up to her about my issues with Kamel and my fears about the future. I lay on the examination table and let her examine me. Shortly after she started, she asked her assistant to leave us alone. She took a deep breath and her face went pale like she was about to tell me I had a tumor of some sort.

"Arwa, are you sure about Kamel's faithfulness? Is it possible that he met someone else right before you got married?" she asked me, stuttering as she spoke. I asked her about the reason behind her question, so she informed me that I had cervicitis, or inflammations on the cervix, that she guessed were transmitted through a sexual encounter, and that I must have gotten it from Kamel. Suddenly, I felt the blood rush to my head like a pumping fountain, like the one he showed me in Dubai before. I remembered Dorreya's words and asked her, "Maybe it was transmitted to him long before our marriage and showed up now?" to which she said that it was an unlikely yet possible option. In the first couple of minutes, all I thought about was him cheating on me but I suddenly began to panic when I fully realized that he might have transmitted a dangerous disease to me.

She tried to reassure me, but I didn't listen to her. Instead, I asked her to run all the possible tests to exclude all possibilities of having any STD. After my persistence and obvious panic, she listened to me and called a friend of hers that owned a nearby lab. We went there together, and her friend took a swab and ran blood tests, then informed me that the results were going to come out in two days. After we left the lab, I asked Nehad to take me somewhere open, so she suggested a quiet, outdoor space that she liked, which turned out to be a garden that belonged to a classic restaurant I had never heard of before. It was soothing, but I was nervous beyond words. She tried to reassure me by insisting that the infection didn't indicate I had other infections elsewhere, and that it was a common one. I didn't detect complete honesty in her words, but I played along and eventually opened up to her about everything that happened since I met with Dorreya.

She tapped her fingers on the table, then tried to make things somewhat lighter by telling me that most men were just like Kamel. I asked her if her husband was the same, to which she smiled sarcastically and said, "Sometimes I wish he was! But then again, I think I deserve a normal husband with normal flaws. Why does it have to be a cheater like Kamel or a careless, uncivil person like my husband?" I asked her, "Do you think he truly loves me?" She smiled bitterly and said, "Of course he does. I'm sure his excessive romance, his gifts, and trips are all ways to make up for the guilt he feels towards you because he probably cheated repeatedly as Dorreya told you he used to. He could be one of those men who don't consider sleeping with whores and heading to strip clubs a form of adultery." She then added, "The medical issue you have is treatable, and I'm sure the tests you ran today will all come out negative. The problem is that anytime he's away from you, you'll start to question whether he's with someone else. Listen, I'm not sure what the perfect advice to give you is. Many women make peace with their husbands cheating on them as long as they make it up for them with love, money, and gifts, or at least they ignore it and pretend it's not there. And of course, you should always make sure you're safe so you won't catch a disease from him again."

What she said didn't make any sense to me. Perhaps it would apply if I had stopped loving him or if many years had passed after our marriage. I knew I had every right to have a baby, but how could I want a child from a man who might transmit a sexual disease to me from one of his whores at any given moment? I couldn't believe I was discussing the possibility of staying with him in the first place, no matter how much we loved each other. His love for me was just an emotional need to fulfill a desire he had, the desire of living a love story. But if he proceeded to cheat on me, then it meant that he wasn't necessarily in love with Arwa, he was simply in love with any given woman. At that moment, I reached a new conclusion. I realized that Kamel had more complicated needs than most men do, as he needed to experience an intense love and live a fiery adventure as if he was still in his twenties. He had a surplus of sentiments that would be sufficient for thousands of cheesy, romantic movies. He craved the look of bedazzlement in the eyes of the women he was with (which is a thing that went away when he was with Dorreya and that will go away after years of marriage). He wanted to experience being with different women. No, I refuse to stay with him, even if I go back to being completely alone or if I marry a less attractive, less romantic, or less financially stable man. I won't accept becoming an ornament that completes Kamel's life, even if I am an expensive piece. I won't accept that he buys my love, because if I do, I will lose a decent amount of self-respect.

14

ZIAD—SOUTH PACIFIC OCEAN, SEPTEMBER 2019

"Head south, go straight ahead, don't swerve to the left or right no matter what you run into, have a big meal beforehand to fill your belly, but not so big that it would slow down your movement, especially since you might pass by orcas and tiger sharks, both of which feed on dolphins. You have to maintain your ability to be able to escape them. As soon as you find yourself in the dead zone, don't waste your time looking for food because you won't be able to find any except by sheer coincidence. You will swim for two whole days amid violent waves before you reach the magical island, and there, you'll find plenty of food."

Those were the old dolphin's instructions one day before going on my trip. I wanted to make up an excuse for my pod so I could leave them for a couple of days, especially since I didn't want to worry my mother or my friends, but the old dolphin advised me against it. He told me to leave without a reason, and when I came back, all I had to do was tell them I got lost or went hunting in a new area. When he noticed my reluctance, he warned me, "Don't tell anyone so they won't insist to join you."

That night, I was overcome with doubts. I spent a long time rethinking my decision and asking myself, "What if the old dolphin was delirious and hallucinating?" When the right half of my brain would go to sleep, my left half would encourage me to go for it, since it's the braver and more impulsive part. It isn't concerned with emotions and doesn't fear consequences, whereas the right part of my brain is more restrained and cautious, like my mother's brain. The interchange between the two halves on that night almost drove me insane, as I impatiently awaited the morning's arrival so my brain could feel clearer and more balanced, with a better capacity to support either one of the two halves.

At that moment, I wished my father was still alive. Would the old dolphin allow me to tell him? Was my father one of the rare, chosen dolphins who could transform into human beings in the first place? Of course he was, or else where did I get this passion from? My mother told me he went out to hunt one day and never came back. Maybe he went to the island and decided to stay there after becoming human, or perhaps he became friends with a group of dolphins that were chosen too. It must be beautiful to be able to live with an entire pod of dolphins who have the same powers, where you could swim together in the ocean as dolphins, then proceed with your lives on the island as humans. There was no way to confirm all those fantasies until I reached the island, experienced being a human, and learned everything about them.

As soon as the sun had risen, I headed out. I made sure the sun was to my left, then I moved south with all my strength. The waves helped me move faster, as they carried me along and pushed me forward. I needed to keep readjusting myself so I could keep moving south. I passed by a boat that carried some humans. They started taking pictures of me and emitting annoying, loud noises, which made me think to myself, "You're going to make me change my mind, you idiots. In what universe is turning into one of you something I'm willing to risk my life for?" The waves kept carrying me while I let my body move on their terms. I noticed the humans point at me in astonishment, as they weren't used to seeing a dolphin swim alone.

I slowed down so I wouldn't drain myself too fast. I carried on swimming at a medium pace underneath the water so I could avoid dealing with the waves and simply continue my path. By that point, I had reached an open space where my echolocation abilities couldn't detect any island or sea barriers. I came across a small flock of fish and devoured some, even though I wasn't hungry, but I did it thinking about the long trip that awaited me. I proceeded to swim at a medium speed for a couple of minutes, feeling grateful for my level in the food chain which allowed me to prey on that fish. A few moments later, however, my ranking in the chain felt inferior when my prey was out of sight, and my predators showed up instead.

A group of orcas was swimming at a nearby distance, with their large bodies colored in black with white undersides. I swam away quietly, trying not to emit any sound in the process, when I suddenly noticed two of them leaving their flock and heading towards me. I was hoping to appear like an insufficient meal that isn't worth fighting for, especially since I was all alone, but apparently, they were too hungry. Therefore, I set out at a great speed. I was able to swim faster than them at the beginning, but they continued to chase me. My tail was beginning to splash more aggressively and squirm more tensely and my speed was starting to slow down, as I could almost smell the gluttony reeking out of their open mouths. In fact, I could almost smell my own blood that was about to be spilled in no time. I wanted to scream at them and declare that I was a special dolphin, not a regular meal. I wanted to announce that the ocean was going to suffer more from losing me than it would any other ten random dolphins, a baby humpback whale, or a group of seals.

One opened its jaw and was ready to aggressively attack my fluke, but I suddenly swerved, swam forward, and jumped in the air while spinning my body and enjoying the warm breeze and drizzle of the ocean. Those leaps were meant to clear my mind and provide me with extra confidence, as I felt the water flow smoothly inside my body. They weren't meant to make me physically faster, but quicker on my feet. The orca also leaped behind me, then went back to the water, creating a large wave that pushed me a couple of meters forward. I used that wave to dive again, while they continued to follow me.

The chase lasted longer than it should have. In a normal chase, the prey usually has an inner conviction that he is meant to fulfill the predator's needs, but of course not just any predator, only one that is worthy of being dominant. That is why a prey intentionally drains it with a long chase, to test out the predator's strength and legitimacy. In my case, while I was being chased by those orcas, I didn't have that feeling at all. I didn't feel like normal prey. On the contrary, I felt like they should be the ones who had to compromise and spend a couple of hours in hunger for my sake. Later, I felt that this strong conviction somehow began to affect them, as they realized I was more than just a piece of flesh that relieved their hunger, and they eventually let me go.

I stayed on my path until nighttime was nearing and the ocean became free of any creatures. I considered diving deeper, but I remembered I couldn't waste any more time. The sun was about to set to my right as I swam just below the surface, going up to the surface to catch my breath from time to time. When it was nighttime, I dove in deeper and swam quietly while getting more and more sleepy. I felt some movement around me, which turned out to be a flock of tiger sharks. I am sure that they considered a dolphin my size a sufficient meal that was worth the chase.

Therefore, my second chase en route to the magical island began. I used all my mental energy to be able to conquer the feeling of sleepiness that was beginning to take over the left side of my brain, which was the side I needed the most at the time. That of course doesn't mean the right side was any less important, since fear and requiring safety were important instincts I needed to hold on to so I could overcome that new obstacle. I set out as far as I could, while they followed me with their infuriating zigzag movements like they were partaking in some satanic dance that aimed to steal my soul. Those hateful creatures proceeded to chase after me for a long time. I have no respect for them, I would rather be devoured by an orca than a lousy tiger shark that resorts to feeding on the ocean's trash and human garbage when they don't find fish. They were, however, more persistent and took a longer time chasing me than the orcas from before did. It seemed like their inferior mental skills would never conclude I was a special dolphin, which is a realization I could swear the orcas had reached. After all, they were our cousins; just larger and more aggressive dolphins.

I attempted to escape them by diving into a deeper level. I desperately kept trying to move downward then swim upward again and jump in the air, riding the waves so I could get further away from them. Soon, I'd find them again nearby, trying to bombard me. Once again, I swam to a deep level then headed upward like an arrow breaking into the air. I spun powerfully with my body, trying to reactivate my mental activities, but when I'd returned to the water, they were suddenly gone. I looked behind me, letting out my sound waves to detect their location. I realized that they got occupied with eating some small sharks, finally freeing me from the long chase.

15

ARWA—CAIRO, JANUARY 2019

I told Kamel my mother wanted me to sleep over at her house to look after her, as I couldn't look him in the eye that night. I still couldn't fully absorb what was going on. He gave me the quality of love I had yearned for all my life; it was a picture of a perfect connection between two lovers that all poets and writers painted, an ultimate ecstasy or a childlike frenzy that lifts you and makes you forget about anything beneath you. Every time he took me on one of our endless tours in those faraway, magical cities, I felt like a child that was being accompanied by her father to an amusement park for the first time in her life, a child who wasn't thinking or worrying about anything. "Dad, I want to go on the Ferris wheel." "Sure, sweetheart." "Hey, Dad, I want pizza." "There you go." "I also want soda and French fries, the ice cream looks good too." "Three scoops of ice cream with three different flavors, just for you!" That's what I felt like: a spoiled little girl whose father takes her to all the amusement parks, beaches, gardens, and places she had ever dreamt of. In the end, however, she's informed that she has to pay for those privileges in sorrow and pain, because her father wasn't going to take her back home, but he was going to throw her under a bridge where she could join the rest of his homeless children.

As soon as I entered my parents' house, my mother started asking questions. I begged her to leave me alone, which of course she didn't. My father asked her the same thing, saying that I was an adult who shouldn't be questioned that way, but she didn't listen to him as she never does when it comes to me. I suddenly raised my voice and yelled at her, "I had a big fight with Kamel! Can you just let me go to sleep or should I go sleep in a hotel? Would that make you happy?" My mom's face went pale as I have never spoken to her that way my entire life. She glanced at my dad and told him to call Kamel since he must have done something that deeply hurt my feelings, but I screamed again and made them promise not to call him. I repeated my dad's words about me being old enough.

I sat in my room in an uncomfortable position to apply the topical medication Nehad gave me. I felt extremely humiliated as if flames suddenly replaced the cream and crawled their way into my organs, swarming up my chest and wrapping my entire body to burn every spot that Kamel has ever touched. It felt as if the disease resided on the tips of his fingers and his lips, and was able to spread all over any area he paid extra attention to. He treated my body as if he was a temple's servant that carried out a holy duty, who bowed down to holy thresholds and carried out submissive rituals. At the end of the day, however, he was a servant who sanctified his gods when he was within their presence but spat on their temples as soon as he left them. I felt a true pain in every spot that he pleased, a harsh, squeezing pain as if every part of my body that was ever pleased by him cringed and denounced him.

I was able to avoid him the following day. On the third day, I got my test results back from Nehad's friend, Hoda. She informed me that everything turned out normal, except for a type of mild bacteria that only needed to be treated with two pills that were to be taken once each. She did, however, confirm that Kamel transmitted the disease to me and that he acquired it recently. She heavily sympathized with me, since Nehad told her what had happened, with my permission. I felt like Hoda somehow considered herself a part of this and that she wanted to take revenge on Kamel for my sake.

I finally went back to our house. Before going back, I was able to avoid him as much as I could in the office, as I claimed I had a lot of work to do, especially since I had been too busy looking after my mom. When I opened the door, he welcomed me with open arms, but I simply avoided his hug and threw at him the test results that Hoda gave me and the report that Nehad wrote about the other infection. At the bottom of Hoda's test results, she had written a note: "sexually transmitted disease." I didn't have to ask him to admit anything since everything showed on his guilt-ridden face as if he had been waiting for those results. I immediately asked him, "How many women did you sleep with, Kamel?" to which he responded with tears in his eyes, "Give me a chance to explain." "I'm just mad you weren't even careful!" I said. He opened his mouth in disbelief, so I continued, "Cheaters like you are usually careful, but to my luck, I fell for a brainless cheater."

I never imagined I could verbally humiliate a man I was married to. Even during the peak moments of disagreements between me and my ex-husband, I never called him a bad word. However, I never carried this weight of hatred and hostility towards him either. Kamel's eyes welled up, as usual, but this time I didn't perceive them as false tears. They were lowly tears that didn't indicate guilt, only the inferiority of their beholder. He confessed to me he made one mistake in Baku when he was with his friends and simply decided to go with the flow, but he was careful as he didn't trust the safety of whores. He got the disease, however, when he slept with a waitress he met here in Egypt while I was busy with my mother at the hospital. She seduced him and they ended up in bed together, but he insisted that he didn't sleep with her on our bed. I laughed bitterly and told him, "How nice of you!" "I wasn't thinking, I got caught up in the moment. I wasn't planning to do it, it just happened anyway," he told me.

He kept swearing and insisting how much he regretted both times, and that he meant to mention they were two times not one as a token of his sincerity and to repent his sins, as he wanted to come entirely clean before starting over, "With Dorreya, I never felt regret when I slept with other women. But with you it's different. I felt horrible guilt, and I wanted to make it up for you even if you didn't know about it." I examined him thoroughly as he felt incredibly small to me at that moment. Every good thing he ever did suddenly vanished. Not only did he cheat on me, but he didn't care enough to protect me or keep me safe, he was the one who put me in that horrible situation. If my gynecologist was someone else other than Nehad, she might have thought I was a promiscuous woman who slept with plenty of men other than my own husband. Even worse, if I had gone to a male gynecologist, he could be one of those lowly types, like Kamel himself, who would assume I was cheap. He might even have tried to seduce me. After all, I am an attractive and cheap woman, who slept with so many men that I contracted a sexual disease. If Nehad wasn't my gynecologist, at least one person in my life would have assumed I was a whore.

"I want a divorce!" I told him. He tried to make excuses and apologies while he was sobbing and wailing all over again, but I had stopped believing in that gullible idea that men's tears are always genuine or unquestionable. Kamel had taught me that men's tears can also lie and deceive, that they can use their tears to play with our emotions and support their lies with the false excuse that men's tears aren't easy. "It's better to have an amicable divorce because I'm taking those reports to court with me and I will ask for compensation." He proceeded to attempt changing my mind, recounting long stories and examples of women who forgave their loved ones, and stressing that men sometimes make mistakes regardless of the degree of their love. "Please tell me how to make it up to you! I'll do anything you want," he said and began to list many options that were going to cost large sums of money, so I said persistently, "I'm not that cheap." "But I'm your husband, so I owe you this!" he said.

He resorted to a new argument, saying he was a rich and young gentleman who could have had any other woman of his choice without exerting half the effort he did for me, yet he still did it because he genuinely loved and wanted to grow old with me. By the end of that long speech I finally told him, "Please look for a hotel to spend the night at and we can continue talking tomorrow. By then, I hope you agree to have an amicable divorce, or I'll have to call my lawyer. That's all I have to say." I left him and headed to my room, slamming the door behind me.

After he left, I called Nehad and told her everything that had happened. She admired my confidence and persistence. In the middle of our call, I received a notification on my phone from the tour agent that was organizing our trip to Tahiti. He was informing me that he booked everything we needed with non-refundable tickets. I laughed out loud reading his message, so when Nehad asked me about it, I said, "Kamel is about to waste $15,000 on nothing." When I told her more about our trip, she said, "Why don't you go on your own? You could use a nice trip without him, may he and all men go to hell." I laughed out loud despite my pain. I then asked her to join me, but she said she was busy with her clinic, husband, and kids. I liked the idea of going alone, as it felt like some sort of revenge on him, especially since he expressed how much he genuinely wanted to spend ten days with me in one of the most beautiful spots in the world. "I'll go!" I told myself. "I'll bathe in the ocean's water and clean off all the heavy weight."

ZIAD—MOTO MUAYA ISLAND, SEPTEMBER 2018

The following morning arrived after a short sleep. I was still in the dead zone, heading south and thinking about the long journey ahead of me. I still had to keep going for an entire morning and night in that massive space of empty water that lacked any marine life, except for the rare inhabitants that existed there. At least I was safe from the orcas and tiger sharks, so I had nothing to fear besides the potential illusion of a magical island that never existed and never wanted me around.

It was a clear morning with smooth water and no currents. I kept switching between swimming at the bottom of the water and jumping above it. Around midday, the waves became higher, so swimming at the surface began to get more challenging. I dove deeper, but when I swam up once more to replenish my air supply, the wind started to shove me around, controlling me the way two dolphins would play catch with a piece of wood for fun. I plunged into the water after taking a short and insufficient breath, as the water current became more turbulent and the waves propagated towards the water surface. Soon, I started to feel like I was suffocating. I tried to float once more, but the wind was extremely aggressive that time, forming a whirlpool that spun me around.

The sun had set, it turned dark, and the whirlpool was still spinning me around above the water. I fought against it so I would be able to dive before I realized that there was a whirlpool inside the water as well. I could feel the air escaping my lungs, while the right part of my brain struggled to remain awake. Even the left side of my brain had a shorter attention span at that point. The whirlpool was still rotating, the wind was controlling me, the water was swallowing then spitting me, while I remained completely helpless. Eventually, my brain went quiet and so did everything else.

I suddenly woke up with all of my senses. The water was calm, the waves gentle, the sky clear, and the sun went down the sky as if I lost consciousness for only a couple of minutes. I was able to smell land, so I turned around and found a rocky cliff that was extremely high and that stood against the water at an upright angle. Its bottom was soft, with algae all over its escarpment, whereas grass spread over parts of its summit. Could it be the magical island? Was it possible that the old dolphin didn't know exactly how long the journey took, or did I lose consciousness for twenty-four hours and a couple of minutes? I doubt it. He probably meant to say two periods of sleep instead of two full nights, which meant that the times I spent sleeping were counted: I slept for a full night last night and a couple of minutes today, that completed two full "nights."

All that nonsense didn't matter anymore, because I knew I had to find an entrance to the island. That rocky cliff appeared endless. "Which direction should I take? Do I get around it from the east or the west?" I asked myself. I decided to head east. It was extremely pleasing to swim there, but I was starving. I couldn't spot any fish on the horizon. I tried to sense the depth using echolocation, but I didn't find anything, so I tried it again and again. Meanwhile, hunger was getting the best of me. After passing a long distance, the cliff was still persistent and endless.

I finally found a shore with plenty of fish swimming near it, but I couldn't catch any of them. And there was the island! Should I take the risk now and throw my body on the shore as the old dolphin told me to? Should I risk my life? What if this was just a normal island after all? I would die like a thoughtless, amateur dolphin that tried to swim in the shallow water but ended up diverting to the shore, then was unable to return to the ocean again.

"You can't achieve glory or individuality unless you take a risk," a voice whispered in my head, followed by the old dolphin's voice as he repeated a human saying, "Whoever fears climbing the mountain, lives his whole life buried underground." I was starting to have my doubts about this sense of glory I was supposed to acquire when I became human. The old dolphin mentioned my identity was going to split into two halves: the identity of the land creature and the identity of the water creature. Was it worth taking the risk? Was it so wrong to live my whole life as a regular dolphin that only lived to enjoy life's simple pleasures? The problem was that even now when I was about to risk my whole life, I still didn't understand how the planet would benefit if I was able to transition into a human. I only had the old dolphin's words for it.

The voice inside me was getting louder and clearer, pushing me closer to the shore. The tide carried me forward as I gave in to it. I was confused, as I didn't resist the voice, but I didn't resist the tide either. Still, I wasn't actively chasing the danger. The waves pushed then pulled me, and on the second push, I was extremely close to touching the shore. I was overwhelmed with my desire to get there, as if the sand had some magnet in it that pulled me towards it.

The following wave was strong enough to forcefully push my body until I fully reached the shore, and that's when I was able to resist the reclining water. When my full body was on land and after the last wave completely receded, I found myself quivering and trembling. I felt my body shrinking and the ground around me getting bigger. Suddenly, I saw arms instead of fins and I felt my growing feet spring and replace my flukes. I was expecting to feel some kind of pain during this transition, but everything was changing right in front of my eyes without any kind of physical pain. It was astonishing to watch my body change and reshape itself, as my eyes normally aren't able to visualize any part of my body. The transition allowed me to turn my head in a new and enjoyable yet frightening way. Moments later, another wave came and touched my lower half, so I felt my fluke returning to what it was, which made me half-dolphin, half-human. When the water receded again, I pushed my entire body inward while crawling on land, until I was far from the water. I then sat down, leaning on my elbows.

I felt my body, face, nose, mouth, and feet. It was an unexplainable feeling that the old dolphin forgot to mention, to be able to touch myself. I grabbed my face with my hands! Us dolphins always feel the need to be touching, that's why we swim so close to one another. What a wonderful feeling it was to hold my head and touch it that way. A voice whispered again inside me, reassuring me and slowing down my racing heartbeats. The old man mentioned that voice too, as he claimed that the spirit of the island whispers what you want to hear, guiding you in your first moments as a new human and brushing the shock away from your enchanted, dazed soul. It also relieved the cells of my body, my tense muscles, and my mixed emotions. It reminded me of a mother's soothing voice to her baby as she guides him on his first moments on Earth, that voice that aids him in inhaling and latching on to the breast, drinking from its milk.

I was still hungry, so I stood on my two feet and walked in the direction of the trees. Oh God, the ground beneath me had a unique feeling, whereas the sand played with my feet's soles the way soft corals soothed a wounded dolphin's body. I reached the very first tree, but I ignored the voice inside me that told me its fruits weren't edible. My feet led me to another tree which fruits were dangling from. I grabbed one and took a bite. It tasted delicious, as it triggered new senses and played with my brain. It was the first taste besides fish that I have ever tried and the first food sensation that triggered the taste buds of my human tongue.

Following the old dolphin's advice, I headed east. My navigation skills were diminished, so I resorted to the sun's aid to determine my direction. I could only see what was included in the realm of my vision, and could only hear what was in the realm of my hearing. To be human also meant that your senses were going to be more limited than usual, but your enjoyment of those senses took you places. The ground felt different underneath my feet; the soft sand massaged them and the green grass tickled them. Sometimes, the tiny pebbles would hurt when I pressed on them, but it was a bearable and intriguing kind of pain at the same time. I was headed towards the residence of the elders at the base of the mountain. The old dolphin explained everything to me: how I was supposed to find three old ladies that were said to be dolphins previously but who knew the secret behind the island, and who were replaced with three others every fifty years. It is also claimed that they are just a representation of the island's spirit.

I felt tired. My feet began to hurt and my head became dizzy while my eyes were overcome with sleepiness. As a human, sleep is meant to take over my whole brain and not just half of it, while both my eyes are meant to be closed, and not just one. I sat on the grass and laid my body on it, but the gravel and wood didn't make me feel comfortable. How strange are those humans! They are sensitive to everything even though their senses are weak and bland when compared to dolphins'. I got up from my sleep, brushed the gravel and dry branches off the ground, then cut some tree leaves and some grass and spread them underneath me. I then laid my body on them and went into a deep sleep.

ZIAD—MOTO MUAYA ISLAND, SEPTEMBER 2018

I woke up to the sunlight that seeped through the leaves of the surrounding trees and tickled my face. The soft, soothing chirps of small birds reached my ears like my mom's gentle whistles when she used to make sure I was fully awake before going on hunting lessons. My throat was dry, which I didn't understand. I listened to the voice inside me that told me to walk so I could find a remedy for that dryness. I spotted a water source: a tiny stream that flowed between the trees. I bent over it, stuffed my mouth with water, and then swallowed it, feeling the liquid run in my throat and consequentially soothing the dryness. I felt a new type of pleasure, another addition to the human pleasures I was beginning to explore.

I glanced at the transparent part of the stream's surface, where I caught my human reflection. My body consisted of two parts, a revealed part where my skin showed a slightly dark color, similar to the skin color of the residents who live in the islands surrounding us, and a second part that was concealed with a grey layer which reminded me of a dolphin's color. I looked like when humans put on one of those suits they wore to dive in the surrounding waters, except that my face, arms, and legs were bare. Apparently, the island hid parts of my body with that suit as part of the ritual. I contemplated my features; I had black sunken eyes, curly black hair, and a prominent, yet not too sharp, nose. In general, I approved of my human shape.

Continuing to walk, I spotted tiny quadruped animals, some running on the ground and others climbing trees. I ignored them since the voice urged me to keep walking and disregard them. Still, they kept surrounding me with their curious glances. I almost understood their whispers, as one of them said, "Here's a new dolphin that just turned human. Let's welcome him," while another one responded, "Why should we? I don't care." I stood at the bottom of a tree, reached out for some fruits, and devoured them, then continued to walk. The pebbles beneath my feet bothered me, so I tried to avoid them and walked on the sand or the grass instead.

I reached the foothill. The voice guided me to walk along a specific direction like it was rerouting my path every time I diverted until I finally reached a small, thick shrub at the bottom of a mountain slope. I entered through the thick leaves while trying to find my way by carefully listening to the voice's directions. A beautiful scent suddenly spread in the air, so I inhaled deeply to enjoy it even more. The smell suddenly intensified, tickling the inside of my nose, until it made me sneeze. It was an unpleasant feeling! I considered how every human pleasure came with a downside. For example, feeling hydrated is always preceded by a dry sensation, smelling a beautiful scent comes with the tickling of the nose then the sneezing, standing upright on sand or grass comes with the exhaustion of the legs, and, of course, the pebbles and other materials I hadn't tried yet would still surprise me even more. After all, I hadn't fully gotten into the human lifestyle yet. I was still an amateur.

"Welcome, Moto Muaya's new son," a voice called out from afar, so I walked further into that space. The lights were dim, but I was able to spot three females, who I guessed were the elders of the island who were about to lead me in my transformation journey. They were sitting together on a tree branch, attached to one another. The one sitting in the middle was the only one speaking, while the others interacted with her physically.

"Finally, you've arrived! You completed the first half of your transformation journey: You believed in the island and were able to arrive here with your skills and capacities," the old woman said. I told her, "Before I ask about my second stage, can I understand what's the point behind all this? How will the other dolphins benefit from this transition?" She chuckled, while her sisters' eyes widened. She said, "You're in such a rush. If only you could wait till the end of your journey, you'll know everything. But if you want to learn now, I can tell you." I agreed, so she said, "The human wisdom, their history and experiences, their pain, dreams, and ambition, are all valuable things that dolphins must learn from so we can maintain our status among other creatures." "How does this maintain our status among creatures?" "Knowledge, my son, is everything. It's the root of wisdom and superiority. To mix this great knowledge and wisdom with the strength of dolphins' strong senses, inclusive hearts, and land experiences will maintain our status forever." She was quiet for some time, then proceeded, "The dolphin that owns this capacity will undoubtedly benefit his species, and he could be among the chosen ones that can live his life as a human among other humans and not just on the island."

"Among other humans! Is that even possible?" I said in shock. "Yes, of course, the human world also needs the feelings and experiences that dolphins know well that they don't, but don't think too much about it. I'm talking about a very rare type, and you probably won't be one of them," she told me. Her words infuriated me. "But I know myself!" I told her. "You're always in a rush, young man. You share more with human beings than you think. There are three conditions for you to be one of the rare ones but now is not the time."

Curiosity ate at me such that I almost begged her to explain more, but she refused. Her excuse was that I couldn't try to reach that level on purpose and that I had to qualify for it without realizing it. "What you need to do now is to climb to the top of the mountain, stand on the high cliff, and throw yourself from up there. Then the island will reveal itself to you." I found her task quite simple, so I left the shrub, headed to the mountain, and began to climb it. It was easy at first, but I soon began to feel exhausted. I looked for a fruity tree among the many trees on the mountainside but to no avail. The voice told me to descend the mountain, feed myself first, then take some fruits with me.

I climbed down, but my human feet tricked me and I tumbled. My body rolled over and fell while the physical pain kept increasing until I finally reached the bottom. Every part of my body was hurting and I immediately noticed scratches and bruises all over my skin, as well as tears on the additional skin-like costume I was wearing (or that the island made me wear). I stood in pain, yearning for the loose corals that soothed my pain and wounds. I headed to the nearest fruity tree, devoured some fruits, and drank plenty of water from the nearby stream. I took some fruits with me and stuffed them between my body and my outer skin costume, then returned to the mountain. The higher I climbed, the more it kept getting harder and the air scarcer. My breathing was getting more rapid with every moment and every step. The sun was about to start setting, but I was determined to reach the top before nighttime. I thought about how I could use some extra sleep in my human form, but I was barely able to breathe due to the insufficient oxygen.

Finally, I was able to reach the peak! The round sun was sinking below the horizon, with a soft twilight that didn't hurt your eyes when you looked towards it. I stood at the edge of the cliff, from which the water appeared extremely far. Its depth was abysmal and the low waves were barely visible from where I stood. There was no going back, it had to be done no matter how terrifying it looked. Whenever I tried to go for it, I pictured the cliff getting even longer while rocky spikes that threatened to tear me apart grew out of it on my way down. I took a deep breath, threw all my fears behind my back, and jumped. I flew in the air, while the wind hit my face and entire body. I closed my eyes and gave in to that new pleasure. To dive in the air is a thousand times more enjoyable than swimming in the water. I only experienced a brief taste of it whenever I jumped out of the water with my pod, but it never lasted that long.

As soon as I touched the water, my body expanded and all the humanly details vanished, getting replaced by the intuitive dolphin senses. As I was able to listen to the ocean's sounds again, my whistling returned and aided me in finding my way and seeing the invisible. A swarm of small fish was approaching, sacrificing themselves to me as a reward, so I devoured them and filled my tummy. I drank from the ocean water, which seeped itself inside me as I had just immersed myself in it. I felt serene, quiet, and full before I turned around with my body and swam back to the island's sandy beach. I threw my body and returned to being human, with a new skin that was free of scratches and bruises, and a new suit that was free of any tears.

I walked on the island towards the grassy parts, while new thoughts invaded my head: dates, dreams, imaginations, visions, thoughts, languages, traditions, rituals, and many shapes and colors of humans. I threw my body once again on the ground and gave in to the muse that flowed in my head like an unstoppable flood. I couldn't tell if the ground beneath me was sandy, grassy, or made of pebbles, as my head was too busy connecting with that muse until I finally fell asleep.

ARWA—EN ROUTE TO TAHITI, APRIL 2019

I stood in front of the buffet at the first-class lounge area for Air France. I added a tiny portion of food to my plate and filled my glass with orange juice before returning to the table I picked, which was in a corner away from everyone. The sun had finally risen after I had spent two thirds of my night on a plane that flew me from Cairo to Charles de Gaulle airport. I was meant to spend twelve hours waiting for my following flight to Los Angeles, which was going to fly me to Papeete, the capital of Tahiti. I had spent three hours sleeping on the plane, so I was about to spend the rest of my waiting time awake in that lounge.

It had been three months since I got divorced from Kamel. Nothing complicated or worth mentioning happened during the process, as the claim I had against him was so disgraceful that he was terrified I might mention it. It turns out he didn't know me well, after all, since the way I was raised would never allow me to publicly speak of such private matters. Even threatening to file a lawsuit against him was nothing more than a threat, I could never picture myself standing in front of a judge and stating my reason behind wanting a divorce.

He tried to negotiate the deferred alimony with me, as he claimed he only had half the money and promised he was going to pay the rest when financial matters improved for him. I didn't argue much, but my father insisted on making him write a check for the rest of the amount, which would require him to pay it within a year of the divorce date. Those negotiations were extremely painful for me as I realized I never felt that level of distress or anxiety during my previous divorce. He shocked me, however, when he headed to the travel agency himself and made them adjust some parts of my trip, like turning it into a solo trip, paying for a first-class ticket, and staying at a nicer hotel. He knew the money was non-refundable, but he didn't have to bend over backward to drastically improve the trip's standards. He probably did it out of guilt, nothing more, like he was trying to earn God's forgiveness for his deeds.

I felt sorry for him. I knew he wasn't ever going to find a woman who truly loved him, and if he did, he was going to lose her even faster than he lost me. Poor guy! I thought he needed to be psychologically treated, perhaps he was denied something as a child and now he experienced that constant gluttony that ended in horrible consequences. Getting him out of my heart wasn't by any means easy, as seeing him at work made me feel nauseous and made my heart race. I eventually asked him to try and remain inside his office as much as he could, and if he needed to ask me something, he simply had to send one of his subordinates to do it.

The lounge became more crowded, even the empty corner where I was sitting eventually became full with the airline's passengers. A family, which consisted of a husband, a wife, and a two-year-old, showed up. The wife sat in the chair next to mine while carrying her child, while the husband went to get them something to eat. I took a glance at the wife, who had loose, dark hair and wore a headpiece with a flower pinned to it. She had very subtle makeup on and light clothing: a plain T-shirt and loose pants that looked similar to sweatpants. She kept her daughter in a pretty stroller. I couldn't determine if she had Arabic roots or not, but I didn't want to further examine her so she wouldn't think I was being nosy.

I got a book out of my bag and intended to spend the rest of the upcoming time with it, until the woman interrupted my reading, asking in a Levant accent, "Are you Arabic?" "Yes, I'm from Egypt." She extended her hand to shake mine and said, "I'm Sarah, from Lebanon." She then introduced me to her husband Ramy and pointed towards the sleeping toddler, "And that's baby Tala." I greeted them openly. She asked about my destination and when I told her, she gasped happily and said, "We're going to Tahiti too." She then leaned in and whispered in my ear about how her husband usually slept too much, so she was happy she found a traveling companion to spend her time with.

I had decided before going on the trip that I was going to let go of my usual rigidness and try to meet new people, possibly build friendships with strangers.

I thought it was a good chance to try new things and enjoy myself for my sake and not for someone else's. I remembered that saying, "Self-love is the closest road to a happy life." Sarah soon opened up to me about her life, her love for her husband, her marriage, and the trip that she's been planning for two years, describing how much she has been pushing her husband to agree to go on the trip. During that time, her husband simply sat busy with his phone and only joined the conversation from time to time to try to justify himself or deny her claims of him being lazy or stingy.

They made a cute couple, reminding me of how Kamel and I used to be and how we made everyone around us envious of our relationship. That damned man was too skilled at being romantic, saying romantic stories, and giving love gazes that exploded with passion. I am sure he wasn't lying or trying to fake that love, but it was still fake. He thought love was nothing but sweet words, romantic songs, excessive attention, and unnecessary money-spending. Those things, however, are just indications of love, they might be performed by anyone even if love didn't own that person's heart. To love is to completely melt in your loved one and let him melt for you, consequentially meaning you won't be able to see anyone else in the world except for him. Your fingertips would refuse to touch someone else even if your brain ordered them to. The first rule of love is "It's all or nothing," meaning that you don't only gift your heart to your beloved, but trust them with all of your body cells. I know that this idealistic picture is rare, but I deserve it. I already had trusted him with all my cells and expected the same thing in return, or at least the basic amount of loyalty.

Sarah was a humorous woman. I was certain that behind that mask of happiness she wore there had to be some problems here and there, but we had just met and I didn't want to drown in her stories or her to drown in mine yet. Her husband did fall asleep during all those hours that we spoke, whereas Tala woke up. She was a beautiful little girl who didn't unnecessarily cry like many babies did; she simply enjoyed herself while playing in her stroller. Sarah had some cereal with her to feed Tala and when I offered to help her, she welcomed the idea. The child quickly got used to me as if she'd known me for a long time, to the extent that after I was done feeding her, I unfastened the buckle clips of the stroller and took her in my arms to put her to sleep.

When Ramy woke up, Sarah suggested that she and I head to the duty-free and leave Tara with him. I expected him to refuse or complain, but he nicely agreed and took the baby. I thought to myself, "Lucky woman!" then I remembered Kamel and considered the possibility that Ramy agreed to do it only because he found the air hostess attractive and wanted to initiate a conversation with her, while poor Sarah assumed her husband was a sweetheart who let her shop without him. "How cynical have I become? Does the poor woman not deserve to be happy? Is every man who treats his wife gently or with extra care a cheater and a hypocrite who doesn't show his true colors? No, of course not," I thought to myself as I stood in front of a line of perfumes while a French sales girl showed us the different brands and sales. I knew some French, but Sarah spoke it like it was her native language.

We only bought a small number of items before we returned. Time passed quickly with them, and we soon headed to the plane that would take us to Los Angeles. I took my fair share of sleep during that trip, especially since the chair next to me was empty, which allowed me to enjoy my space. Halfway through the trip, which lasted twelve whole hours, Sarah showed up with Tala to keep me company and they sat in the empty chair next to me. We chitchatted for a while and watched a movie until we eventually reached the Los Angeles airport. After a two-hour transit, we rode another plane which landed in Tahiti's national airport at around 8 a.m., while I could barely keep my eyes open. Despite my exhaustion, I didn't miss out on the island's enchanting views that I initially caught from the plane's window. I saw long beaches with incredible greenery that were only accompanied by small white buildings that looked, from above, like snowflakes that covered a large green garden.

Each of us headed to our own hotel, promising each other to meet again. I got into the taxi that the hotel had sent me, feeling nauseous and struggling with a headache. Maybe it was the jetlag! I wasn't thinking about Kamel at that moment, as I was too busy examining the island, the mountains, the greenery, and both the domestic and international tourists. Despite my overall exhaustion and dissociation due to the long trip, I was watching everything with great excitement and longing for better days that would erase my sorrow.

ARWA—TAHITI, APRIL 2019

My first day began with a cloud of discomfort and unease that resulted from my disrupted biological clock. I tried to sleep as soon as I arrived at the hotel but to no avail. I tossed and turned in bed for almost two hours, during which I only snoozed for few minutes, before I eventually got up and decided to head to the beach. There, I sat on the black sand that covered the coast, while resting my body under the shadow of a leaning palm tree that looked like it wanted to look out over the sea instead of the skies. It wasn't the only palm tree that tilted that way, as I noticed they were quite common both at the hotel's beaches and in other ones as well. To my right, there was a valley filled with trees, and I spotted additional faraway mountains that looked like they belonged to a different island.

I got up and stretched out my body upon a plastic chaise longue, then covered my face with a towel and shut my eyes as an attempt to sleep by the fresh, ocean-scented breeze. It worked out; I managed to go into a deep and tranquil sleep that was the complete opposite of my restless sleep in the room. The fresh breeze was much more effective than any pill or herbal drink, at least in my experience. I woke up to a waiter serving me a tropical drink garnished with a fruit slice on top, so I picked up my phone and took a picture of the colorful drink with the lush valley appearing in the background; it reminded me of one of those travel ads' photos. I then uploaded it on my Instagram with a short caption underneath it. Since I hadn't blocked Kamel yet, I expected him to see the picture and be eaten up with jealousy towards everything he was missing out on. I received a notification from Naglaa, who expressed her fascination with the picture, followed by another notification from Nehad who commented, "Put your phone down and enjoy yourself! Forget everything and live your life, girl!"

It was past midnight in Egypt, but it was a Friday night, which explained why everyone was awake. I received another comment from Sarah, "Love the view, but nothing compares to the bungalows here." I smiled to myself, as I knew she had been dreaming for years to stay at one of those bungalows—which were basically overwater huts. She tried to convince me to cancel my reservation and join them, but I told her I had already reserved one in Bora Bora and that I was heading there in two days. She then sent me a picture of herself dipping her daughter's toes in the water with their beautiful hut appearing in the background. Her daughter looked serenely joyful and excited to be touching the water; that picture made me curse my first husband, Kamel, and all the other men who let me down and denied me such a magical moment.

I turned off my phone and decided to leave it in the room's safe for the rest of the day, as I felt the need to abandon any sort of communication with my real world. After doing that, I sighed in relief and headed to the pool, which was on a hill above the beach. I submerged myself entirely in it, letting myself enjoy the water and the scenery. I didn't leave it even when it was time for lunch, I simply asked the waiter to get me a sandwich and a coffee. He brought them to me and placed them on the edge of the pool, so I had them quickly while embracing the lightness of letting go of my world's heavy weight.

Right before sunset, Tahitian traditional dances were scheduled to take place on the black-sanded beach. I heard the sound of the accompaniment, then entered a line of men who wore skirts made of white strings and rectangular headdresses ornamented with feathers and colorful designs, in addition to bright necklaces around their necks. A line of women then appeared; they wore similar-looking skirts but were decorated with shredded palm tree bark and matching bras. Their headdresses had longer feathers that were ornamented with yellow bows and they wore even more colorful necklaces. Overall, they appeared much more flamboyant than the men. The dance went on and on, while their lines intermingled with one another. They looked like they were genuinely enjoying the moment as if they were dancing for themselves and not to a group of curious tourists. The most exciting part was when three long, pointy boats joined the dance. They each had men that were rowing and others who raised flames. The three boats moved smoothly on the water as if they were organically moving on their own.

The following day, I was meant to go on a tour that took us to the most significant monuments of the island. I had postponed my marine trip to Bora Bora and decided to enjoy the beauty of Tahiti. The tour had five other people with me, an American couple and a French man who sat beside me as if we were the third couple on the bus. The tour guide spoke in English after the French gentleman said it was okay. We arrived at our first site, the temple of "Arahurahu Marae." When the tour guide pronounced its name for the first time, he asked me to repeat it after him, but I laughed while trying to get it right, "Can't you abbreviate the name? Maybe remove the 'Ahu' at the end?" I asked. "Of course not, every letter in the name stands for something." That sacred site was a large garden that had two stone structures of fat, primitive-looking figures that were called "Tiki." The tour guide clarified that they weren't original pieces, and that original ones could be found in the museum.

He let us roam the place for a while. I reached a raised area built of black stones spotted with white tints, which surrounded a muddy space that was adorned with flat, wooden puppets that were sculpted in a way that made them look like faces with feathers on the top of their heads. As I was watching them, the French gentleman stood beside me and said, while pointing at a higher raised area, "That's the 'Ahu' that you wanted to remove from the temple's name." I didn't understand what he meant, so he said, "That's the altar where they offered their sacrifices, it's called 'Ahu.' As for 'Marae,' that's what the word temple means in their language."

He was trying to explain the complicated name to me as an attempt to initiate a conversation, which I didn't mind. The idea of a Western man who spoke respectfully to a woman without any sneaky intentions behind his words or actions was something I welcomed. "I'm Fabien, from Toulouse," he introduced himself. "I'm Arwa, from Cairo, Egypt." "Ah, that's why you look so familiar. You look like Nefertari, the queen from ancient Egypt." I thought to myself, "You're not so easy after all, Mr. French guy," then smiled at his compliment. I didn't know who Nefertari was, to be honest. It would have been simpler if he had said " Nefertiti."

He asked me if we could walk together around the temple, to which I agreed. He had a strong background on the site, as he proceeded to explain how Tahiti is located in French Polynesia, one of the sprawling possessions of France. He found that unacceptable, as he supported the idea that it should become an autonomous country. He quickly noticed my face was starting to go blank, as I usually grow bored of geography and politics, so he went back to explaining the things we saw in the temple.

We reached our second stop, Tahiti's Maraa Grotto, which was a cave surrounded by thick forests and ferns. You entered it through a pond in which water fell from the roof. I separated myself from Fabien and walked around the area on my own. The air was untypically chilly, so I went back to the surrounding greenery. Lots of chickens roamed the place and were fed by tourists. I opened my phone to take a couple of pictures, then looked up pictures of Queen Nefertari, who he claimed looked like me. "Yeah, right!" I said to myself. She looked nothing like me, especially since the only available picture of her was the side of her face carved on stone, which didn't reveal her facial features, unlike Nefertiti's statue for instance. Men were simply made of lies, whether they were Egyptian or French.

The tour continued—we went to a garden filled with ponds, plants, wooden bridges, lush trees, ducks, and a small waterfall. That waterfall was nothing fascinating compared to the ones we saw in our following station: the Faarumai waterfalls. After walking for a short amount of time with Fabien, during which we engaged in a conversation, I spotted a high waterfall that appeared as if it flowed right down from the skies, while two other smaller waterfalls flowed next to it. The flow was calm and plunged into a shallow pond.

Everyone in the group was staying at the same hotel as me. We all had dinner together, where Fabien told me more about his job. He was a history teacher, but he was studying for his master's degree in highlands and islands. "I went on this trip for my studies, but I intend to enjoy every minute of it as much as I can," he said in English with a French accent. He said that last sentence while staring right into my eyes, so I smiled somewhat sarcastically and said, "So do I." "Are you seeing someone?" I laughed out loud and said in Arabic, "Come on, not you too." Anywhere in the world, men sniff out women and they don't care who she is or where she's from as long as she ends up with him in the bedroom at the end of the night. That's all that goes on in a man's head, no matter how progressive or respectful he looks. Fabien or Kamel could both be somewhat different in terms of how eloquent and intelligent they were, but all men think about the same thing at the end of the day.

He shook his head, not understanding what I just said in Arabic, so I said, “I’m a queen, remember? I can’t be with a commoner.” He laughed at my joke and said, “So you’re single?” “It’s complicated. Anyway, I’m heading to Bora Bora tomorrow.” He looked disappointed, which I didn’t think was genuine. I excused him and headed back to my room, stretching out on my bed. I had a smile on my face, thinking about the long, beautiful day and how it was worth the exhaustion I felt. I remembered Fabien’s flirtation attempts and smiled confidently because even though I didn’t welcome his flirting or even accept it without a direct response, it still affirmed the magic of my femininity and how it surpassed continents. That’s of course if I had any magic left in me.

ZIAD—BORA BORA, APRIL 2019

Throughout the following months, the island bestowed a brand-new world upon me. I visited it every week after a trip that only took a couple of hours, at the end of which I would always be attacked by a whirlpool that swallowed me, then pushed me closer to the island. There, I gave in to the waves which ended up throwing me on the shore, where I eventually transformed into a human. I would proceed to live an isolated human life: picking fruits and hunting down rabbits to skin then grill them using the flames of fire I created. Then I would enjoy their delicious grilled taste.

I once considered eating grilled fish, but to hunt a living one wasn't an easy task by any means, since I would always turn back into a dolphin as soon as my body touched the water. One time, I grabbed a fish with my jaw without grinding it with my teeth. It was still alive, trying to escape. However, as soon as I got out of the water and turned human, I couldn't handle the sensation of carrying it in my mouth, so it easily slipped and swam back to the water.

On every visit, the island would teach me new things about the human world, from which I would gain additional wisdom by learning more about their actions and the consequences thereof. Their history truly is rich, and their ability to write down history is what differentiates them from the rest of the creatures. It is their greatest skill and the most significant thing I acquired from the island. Their languages are astonishing, too. I had already learned ten, and I was about to learn more in the upcoming days.

The notion of different languages was a unique pleasure for me. Even though the language shared by the dolphins is relatively progressive, it only relies on conveying direct or basic information. The difference in complexity between humans' languages and dolphins' language is analogous to the difference between their history and ours. Dolphins also have a long history, but it mainly consists of basic experiences, instinctive responses, and so forth. We inherited many lessons from our ancestors that led us to improve the survival skills of one generation after the other. We learned when tornadoes would take place or violent winds would strike and we learned many things about predicting them. We learned about the behaviors of both humans and the rest of the ocean's creatures. We knew the migration and mating seasons of fish, we learned how to mate, reproduce, and look after our offspring. Not all of these things are natural and innate instincts, many of them we inherited from our ancestors and each generation adds an extra small amount of knowledge. It is similar to the growth process of knowledge that humans have, but of course, humans have the language that helps them protect and improve that knowledge in a way that can be analyzed, adjusted, and advanced.

My duty began after my first visit to the island. The other rare ones and I tried to utilize this human knowledge to the best of our ability to benefit our species. We weren't sure, however, what had to be taught and what was to be ignored. The old ladies told me I was going to know with practice and through the different situations that we got exposed to as dolphin pods, be it during swimming, hunting, or interacting with individuals or flocks. There were always events happening during which we had to use part of our knowledge or wisdom by conveying it to our pods.

It was crucial to keep the story of the island and my transformation a secret, so the old dolphin told my pod I was chosen to take private lessons with older and wiser dolphins, which was meant to explain my constant and repetitive absences, in addition to the wisdom I gained day after day. When you become a "wise dolphin," you stray away from mating or having a partner, as a cloud of dignity forms around you and leads all the other dolphins to go to you whenever they are facing problems or disagreements.

What I didn't expect, even though the old dolphin had informed me about it beforehand, was that my life pre-transformation had begun to feel like an old, faraway memory. It was just one memory among countless other memories of human lives, histories, and experiences that

I carried along with me. I thought about my mother and Maya of course, and sometimes I felt nostalgic for my old memories with them, but it felt like a nostalgia for something that took place hundreds of years ago. The old dolphin had informed my mother that I had become a wise dolphin, and I learned, through the spirit of the island, that she welcomed the news with pride and joy, as everyone else in our pod congratulated her.

What truly took over my brain, despite all those special privileges I enjoyed, was that some dolphins among the chosen ones could transform into a human on any given land, and not just on the island. To be able to intermingle with other humans outside of the island; what a mesmerizing ability. Even though those creatures had always terrified me, especially after I learned about their history, I still wanted to try out a life among them. To me, it sounded like an intriguing experience that triggered my driven and fearless self.

I had visited the elderly ladies' cave earlier and found them sitting the same way as before as if they were waiting for me. I paid my respects, then sat in front of them and asked, "How do I know I'm the crème de la crème?" The elderly lady said, "You will know when it's time!" "What are the conditions then?" I begged her to tell me. The lady on the right looked pleasantly surprised, whereas the one on the left frowned in disapproval. The main lady, sitting in the middle, said, "This knowledge will bring you unnecessary responsibilities. Knowledge isn't always a blessing, son." After some insistence on my part, she finally said, "The only condition is that fate must choose you, not the other way around. You have to save a human from dying and bring her to the island. She has to be dying and no one can rescue her except you, that's the first condition." I then said, bored with her lingering, "Please carry on. What's the second condition?" "Wait, you need to hear the rest of the first condition: this human has to be a woman. A sorrowful woman who went through a traumatic event, and she has to be single."

I stayed silent for some time, then asked her again to tell me the second condition. "The two of you have to genuinely love each other," after which I thought to myself, "Come on! Why do I have to get into that mess that humans pay such an excessive amount of attention to: relationships?" The most complicated thing that I failed to understand about humans was the love between a man and a woman, which I perceived to be completely useless. No one was able to find a possible explanation for it, and yet all languages and cultures agreed to write about it, cry about it, sometimes even die for it.

Love is an unrealistic sentiment that resurrected your soul, as a result of a bond between you and another being that you have no blood relation with; a sentiment capable of making you commit acts beyond logic. What an irritating condition it was! Even finding a single, sorrowful lady who was about to die in the vast, large ocean was easier than falling in love. "And what's the third condition?" I asked, to which she laughed sneakily and said, "The third condition only applies after the first two. You have to bury both your body and hers under the island's sand, with only your faces revealed, and you let the island determine the third condition."

A while after this visit, I focused on roaming around the ocean, especially in areas where humans usually hang around. Sometimes, I jumped near their boats and played with them, while studying their reactions. They all appeared quite naïve to me and they all perceived me as a performer in a circus or a zoo. I listened carefully to their conversations, how they claimed I was intelligent, friendly, and playful and how they gasped in astonishment whenever they saw me spin my body in the air, which is something any regular dolphin can do. I paid even more attention to women, in hopes of possibly catching a sad, lonely lady before she got herself in danger, then escaping with her towards the island. My fixated attention on women made those humans laugh at me, confirming that I was a male and that I was a womanizer. I repeated the same thing day after day, until one day, I found a woman in Bora Bora who was waddling across the area between the main island and mid-ocean ridge, riding what humans called a "jet ski" by herself. As soon as she spotted me, she smiled calmly. She didn't cheer or yell annoyingly like most of them do, she simply welcomed me as if she was meeting up with an old friend.

I swam around her calmly, but I didn't try to show off any acrobatic movement or a high jump. I rested my rostrum and flippers on the side of her jet ski, so she extended her hand and ran it across my back. It was the first time I came that close to a human and it was a gentle touch but that didn't mean anything. Perhaps if any other human had touched me, I would have felt the same way. Perhaps a human's touch had a different effect from a dolphin's flippers approaching mine.

She suddenly did something unexpected: she got off her jet ski while leaning on me and got into the water, which is an uncommon thing for a human to do. Usually, they believed that direct interaction with a dolphin had to only be performed by professionals who were experienced with marine creatures, or at least it had to be supervised. Despite my shock, I responded to her calmly, as I kept spinning around the jet ski while she leaned against me, swimming with me. She spoke in Arabic, "If only you could help me dive." I didn't think for long and immediately started to dive, but she didn't follow me. I swam up to the surface, approached her, placed my flippers on her hand and then dove slowly so she could join me, but she let go of me. "Stupid humans! Of course she's not going to be the only exception," I thought to myself. I swam up again and placed my flippers on her hand once more, so she said, "You want us to dive together?" I gently rubbed my head against her and whistled, as if I was displaying my agreement. "No way! Did you understand what I meant?" she asked me. She then strongly grabbed my fin, took a deep breath, then dove with me, while holding me with both her hands.

ARWA—BORA BORA, APRIL 2019

The plane's landing in Bora Bora felt like a separate trip. The aerial view revealed a green mountainous island in the middle, surrounded by a grand green arch. Many extensions came out of that large arch, and I was meant to be staying in one of the huts built on one of those extensions. The lagoon's multicolor ranged from a white shade slightly stained with greenery to pistachio to bright blue and finally dark blue, which stretched from the edge of the arch to the massive ocean.

The plane landed on a runway area that reminded me of the Egyptian agricultural road, as it was narrow and paved with greenery on both sides. I headed straight to my hotel, where one of the staff workers guided me along a narrow passage above the water that was surrounded by huts on both sides; mine was at the very end of that pathway. From the inside, it looked like a fancy five-star hotel with an unusual interior design and a mono-pitched, cone-shaped ceiling. The terrace was a different story: a tiny part was set under the wooden pent roof, whereas the rest of it stretched out to the water. It offered a view of Mount Otemanu, where you could see the greenery embrace the clouds as if it generously provided the grass with water without having to wait for the rain to fall.

I spent my whole day inside the room and on its terrace. I swam in the water and enjoyed the soft tickling of the colorful fish that fed on the remnants of my body's impurities. After I got out of the water, I had lunch in front of the mountain's view outside of the room, then decided to stretch my body and start reading one of the novels I brought along with me. None of them were romantic novels, they were either crime, horror, or thriller.

I decided to start with a book called *Gone Girl*[22], an enjoyable novel that was adapted into a successful movie that I had already watched, but I still wanted to read the novel to further understand the writer's raw thoughts and enjoy the female protagonist's ability to control, terrify, and punish—even murder—men. It was how I dealt with my suppressed anger while still relishing the water, the greenery, and the delicious food, especially fish. The spices also were quite unique.

I spent the following day between the beach, the hotel, and the city center. By the end of it, I surrendered underneath the hands of the masseuse. The third day was the day of the scheduled trip, where we were meant to first go on a tour along the lagoons with our jet skis, then we were supposed to enjoy the natural landscape of the area and watch the bays and the islands. After that,

[22] a 2012 crime thriller novel by American writer Gillian Flynn

we were meant to have lunch and go on a cruise during which we were to dive and watch the fish, especially stingrays and sharks.

The tour guide gave us some instructions first. I smoothly and courageously rode the jet ski after I put on my life jacket and diving mask so I would be able to open my eyes when the jet ski went fast. Even though it was my first time riding a jet ski, I moved fearlessly as I had promised to let go of all my fears beforehand. The rest of the participants in the tour were a bit uncomfortable with the idea of swimming with sharks, except me. We set out slowly at first, before getting speedier. I felt like I was flying as the water and wind hit my face. I considered turning around suddenly and simply falling in the water, or perhaps setting out at the highest speed towards any navigational aid then jumping with my jet ski above the signal. I thought about flying up in the air then turning over and bouncing like a stone that people skip across the water. I wanted to act as irrationally and recklessly as I could, but I simply listened to the tour guide's instructions despite my crazy fantasies.

We had stopped with our jet skis in one of the bays when something strange happened: when I was contemplating the area, away from the rest of the group, I found a dolphin approaching me. It appeared as if it was smiling at me with a welcoming attitude, so I smiled back. The guide had mentioned that dolphins showing up in that area would be rare, and what was even stranger was that it was swimming alone. It approached me and kept spinning around me, rising above the surface and then diving in my direction.

I reached out my hand to touch him. I knew it was prohibited to do that with no professional trainer around, but I decided to go for what I wanted. The dolphin approached me with its head, and suddenly I was overwhelmed with desire to get in the water and swim with it. I turned around and realized that the guide was busy with the rest of the group, so I carefully went into the water. I leaned on the dolphin and he smoothly swam with me around the jet ski. I said, "If only you could help me dive" and to my surprise, the dolphin stopped moving. It felt like he was surprised by my request, as if he somehow understood my Arabic language. He placed one of his slippery flippers on my hand, but it easily slid when he dove into the water. He went up again and proceeded to whistle loudly while moving its fluke faster than usual. I thought to myself, "Could it be that you understood me?" It rubbed its head on my chest like a pet cat, then placed his flipper on my hand more firmly until I could feel its strong grab. "Do you want me to dive?" I asked, so he whistled one more time. I turned around to make sure the guide wasn't paying attention, then I turned around, held on to the dolphin's fin strongly, and dove with it while still grabbing on to him.

The mask enabled me to see what was beneath the water, and the dolphin was intelligent enough to dive only near the surface as if it was taking me on a tour. The life jacket bothered me, so I mounted the dolphin's body like a horse and grabbed it even more strongly with my arms and legs. It swam as if we had been doing this all our lives, it rose and dove smoothly then jumped up in a way that made me happily squeal. The jet skis approached us and I heard the tour guide's voice protesting and yelling. He then jumped in the water and swam towards me and the dolphin carefully. The dolphin stopped, as if he understood the tour guide's protest, then it let me slip off of him and swam away quietly.

"You just broke the safety rules, ma'am. I can end your tour now without even refunding your money," the tour guide yelled angrily as he helped me get back on the jet ski. I didn't get back at him, because I was either going to laugh or call him a bad word, nothing in between. We continued the tour, I on my best behavior after I was able to steal a short amount of fun that was even more enjoyable because it was unexpected and against the rules. It felt like I got out some of the suppressed reckless energy I had those days, and I was overjoyed with a sense of unusual ecstasy that continued during our ride back. I was still recalling the fish I was swimming with while being physically attached to another marine creature.

We returned to the beach and had lunch in a restaurant that looked upon the Otenamu Mount from an angle that highlighted a new side of its two-headed peak; one pointy and the other flat. The group I was with was a friendly bunch, the friendliest of whom was an elderly Australian couple, over sixty years of age. They talked to me as if they were talking to their own daughter. As we were waiting for our food, the guide went to talk to one of the restaurant's workers, when the woman told me quietly, "You were wrong, my child. You scared him." I frowned as I didn't understand what she meant, so she said, "The tour guide's responsible for our safety. Those marine animals aren't always safe to interact with, and that innocent dolphin was untrained at the end of the day. He could have hurt or drowned you." "I didn't mean to cause trouble, Deborah. I wasn't thinking about that kind of responsibility," I said apologetically. Her husband said, "I think you should apologize, at least tell him something nice."

I followed Deborah and William's advice and apologized to the tour guide when he returned. He accepted my apology and in return apologized for overreacting. We all ended up eating lobster with white sauce, which tasted completely different from the one I usually eat. We had coconut for dessert after we took a quick lesson on how to open them. After that, we went on another trip, taking a motorboat to the diving area, which was full of diverse marine creatures, especially stingrays, small sharks, and colorful tortoises. Despite all the confirmations that the sharks in that area weren't dangerous, I still had goosebumps when I spotted one of them approaching me. The tour guide patted me on the back for support. I swam with the surprisingly friendly stingrays, and for a couple of minutes, I swam with the colorful tortoises that reminded me of the ones in *Finding Nemo*.

For some reason, I had a feeling that the dolphin from before was still around. I didn't see him, but I was fully convinced he was around and watching. I asked the worker from the hotel to find me someone who knew how to handle dolphins, but of course, I convinced him to do it by paying him. I was even able to convince him to take me to the same spot where I met the dolphin for the first time. I felt like I wanted to swim with him again; a strange feeling that had no explanation besides that I felt empty on the inside and want to follow any unusual adventure to fill the gap. It wasn't enough for me to swim with the dolphin, and I thought it was a spectacular opportunity that I found one that was so accommodating and friendly.

At night, I met with Deborah and William on the beach, where a local band played Pacific music and men and women wearing colorful clothes, even brighter than Tahiti's performers, danced. They offered me to join them on a hike, to which I agreed, but I asked them to make it in the afternoon because I had planned a small trip in the morning. "What trip?" William asked, so I said, "A quick diving lesson." He was about to ask me for details, but Deborah changed the topic and suggested that three of us go together on a trip to watch whales. "I wish, but my budget won't allow me," I said, laughing, but she clarified that the boat was owned by one of their friends and that it was a large group of people who wouldn't mind if I joined. I tried to get out of it before William told me, "You are the same age as Sophie and you remind us a lot of her, so I'm sure you won't mind making our hearts happy by joining us?" I smiled, after not finding any reason to refuse. I left them at night, promising to meet them the following afternoon.

22

ZIAD—BORA BORA, APRIL 2019

I felt that my encounter with that woman was cut short. I was enraged by the tour guide's interference and almost displayed this frustration publicly, but the wisdom I had recently gained from the island inspired me to retreat quietly. I decided to show up the following day in the same spot, which I knew didn't make any sense. She was an Arabic woman, which I learned as soon as I heard her talk. That meant she was a foreigner visiting from the other side of the world. She was probably here for a short time, which meant she wanted to visit as many sites as she could; it didn't make sense for her to visit the same place twice.

It never occurred to me before that I could feel so safe and … some other mysterious feeling I couldn't find a suitable description for. Even though I had learned all those different languages, some things were too difficult to be described with words, especially the feeling I experienced when I was touched by that woman and when she joined me in the water till we eventually became one entity that swam together underneath the ocean's surface. It was simply a new, refreshing feeling; that was all I knew. I thought I could perhaps learn more about it after I returned to the island.

I arrived at our spot the following morning, but I wasn't sure what time exactly I saw her. I learned that humans invented clocks to split time into smaller units, but I didn't have access to one. I kept swimming round and round, and I even caught two fish out of boredom. A different group of people passed by, letting out their usual immature screams and ingenuine gestures. None of them interacted with me the way she did; I believe she was the only one that saw something different in me.

A long time passed during which I continued to swim in circles and roam the same area. Humans claim that time passes slowly during anticipation or wait, and it was my first time to experience that feeling. Ever since I touched the island for the first time, I discovered that whenever something pleasant happens to humans, another thing has got to ruin it in return. She, however, finally showed up. This time, she was in a boat accompanied by a man. Her skin was tanned, making her appear darker than the previous day. She was leaning on the bow of the boat while fixating her eyes on the water. I knew she was undoubtedly looking for me. When she finally found me, her smile widened and her face lit up. She spoke to the man sitting with her in English, saying, "I swear it's him!" whereas the man insisted there was no way it could be me. I wanted to scream at him and yell, "Believe her, you idiot."

I learned that her name is "Arwa." When the man was trying to convince her that he had to get in the water before her for safety purposes, he addressed her as "Miss Arwa." I tried to endure their long discussion and pretend I was just a normal dolphin swimming around. He finally jumped in the water, carefully approached me, then placed his hand on my body until he made sure it was entirely safe to be around me, before allowing her to get in the water and swim with me.

Arwa wrapped her arms and legs around my body the way she did the previous day, attaching herself even more closely to me. We swam around the boat in circles, while the man proceeded to warn her against diving with me or he wasn't going to join her the following day. When he said that, I was overwhelmed with joy, as it took over my body from my fluke to my beak. I jumped up in the air with joy, to which she squealed happily. She said, in Arabic, "You're amazing!" I swam with her in zigzags, the way sharks do, while she continued to laugh happily. The man was still yelling at her to be careful with me. She suddenly said, "Let's dive." I considered listening to her, but I didn't do what she said. I wanted her to show up the following day, and I was too scared they might prohibit her from doing that if we dove together.

"Oh, so you want me to come tomorrow! Do you understand English too? Did you understood his warning, then?" she spoke to me. I felt the urge to reply to her in her language, but I simply whistled gleefully instead. "If you understood me, let's jump!" she said, and I did what she said. "Oh my God! No way!" she exclaimed. At that moment, I wanted to leap in the air and make a full spin with my body, but I didn't know how to ask her to hold on tightly to me. I thought about it, then jumped twice consecutively, making sure the second jump was higher. I repeated the pattern until she eventually understood that every time I jumped twice, the second time would be higher, so she held on more strongly on every second jump. I thought to myself, "She's intelligent!" I gradually increased the elevation of every second jump, until I was finally able to leap extremely high while spinning around myself in a way that allowed me to sense her own pleasure as if it was transmitted through the air.

Our encounter came to an end. She mentioned that she was coming back the following day at a later time, which she did. That time, however, she came prepared. She had a diving suit on and she had other equipment with her, while another man joined her in a diving suit as well. She got into the water and swam with me, while I heard the man expressing his astonishment at the unique bond between us, "I've seen similar bonds between trainers and their dolphins, but not between a regular person or a visitor who was only around for a couple of days."

Arwa spoke to me, claiming that she decided to dive with me. "You cost me a lot of money, but the time I spend with you is dream-like." The man laughed, "What's the use of speaking in Arabic? Even if it was a trained dolphin, it can only understand the language it was trained in." Arwa wrapped her arms around me, held on tightly, and asked me to dive, after she adjusted all her diving equipment. I swam with her to the depths of the water, as I attracted flocks of colorful fish and tortoises to join us in our dive using my whistles. We then approached the barrier reef, so I took her on a tour around the coral reefs and its creatures. All of this took place above a depth of three meters, as I wanted to avoid scaring her or her accompanying coach.

I felt her trying to pull me upwards; she'd had enough of deep diving and wanted to go back to the surface. It was a mutual desire. Underneath the water, we only watched other creatures: fish, tortoises, shark, stingrays. When we jumped above water, however, we could see each other and feel each other's joy, excitement, and many other feelings that even my deepest understanding of human languages couldn't describe.

After we swam up to the surface, she said, "One minute," which I didn't understand. However, I saw her getting on the boat, taking off the diving equipment, then she jumped back in the water and approached me. She grabbed my head, contemplated me with her big eyes, then held my head against her chest. I experienced a sudden chill and couldn't help but rub myself against her like an affectionate pet cat, before I swam beneath the water and swam forward, waiting for her to grab me so we could swim together.

When I jumped in the air that time, it felt as if she was a fellow dolphin enjoying herself with me. I jumped upward while flipping and twisting while she remained attached to my body. On the outside, we resembled two professional dancers performing on stage. That isn't exactly an exaggeration, as some tourists gathered around us with their jet skis and watched us perform our exotic dance, while some curiously asked about the identity of the woman who was that professional at dealing with dolphins. Some even asked her for a chance to swim with me.

After we were done, the spectators clapped and cheered for us in their typically annoying, human way. That time, however, I enjoyed their cheering. Arwa let go of me after telling me she was going on a marine trip the following day and that she hoped she could see me again. The coach smiled sarcastically, confirming once again that talking to me was useless, but she didn't care about him. She mentioned something about visiting the humpback whales. I knew where those visits usually took place, so I decided to meet her the following day and join her in swimming with the whales.

ARWA—SOUTH PACIFIC OCEAN, APRIL 2019

In the middle of the vast, endless water, darkness swallowed the upper half of my body while the ocean devoured my lower half. My lifejacket kept me afloat for longer than I could count, yet I couldn't feel my feet, as if they no longer belonged to my body. I couldn't hear anything except the crashing of the waves, which carried me up and down. The waves' force gave me hope about possibly getting pushed towards the shore, but that hope vanished when I noticed how the land appeared even further than the scattered stars in the moonless sky.

Could it be that my life was coming to an end just after I had enjoyed three of the best days of my life? The highlight of those days was my indescribable bond with that exceptional dolphin that had become like an old friend only a couple of minutes after our first encounter. It cost a fortune to see him again on the following days, but it was worth it. I had never felt that kind of bliss before I met him; it was the kind of happiness that was free of any regrets about the past or expectations for the future. I was simply having a nice time and stealing a sense of ecstasy from the usual worldly momentum and the noise and deceit of people. I savored the moment, stored it inside my heart, and soared with it away from the destructive memories and deep pain.

I gave him the name "Ziad": a name I had always planned to call my future son. As a child, I had always written down that name underneath pictures of babies and as an adult, I mentioned that name to every man I dated. Men would come and go, but the name "Ziad" remained preserved for my imaginary son, whereas the name "Lama" was kept for my future daughter. On our second encounter, which happened in the presence of an expert who assured me it was a male dolphin, Ziad somehow taught me to grab him tightly before he performed his acrobatic leaps. It felt like he was instructing me as a professional swimming veteran would.

I spent the rest of that morning hiking with William and Deborah, then I introduced them to my parents on the phone as the lovely couple who treated me like their own daughter. The following day, I returned to Ziad's spot with the diving instructor as I wanted to dive with him for a longer time. Everyone watching us was amazed at how close we were and how we physically interacted with one another in complete harmony, both above and underneath the water. Their astonishment reached its peak when we performed our last swimming dance together. Before leaving, I told Ziad that we were whale watching the following day; I was sure he understood what I said despite the trainer's mockery of how I dealt with that special dolphin.

At night, I met up with William and Deborah again. We had dinner together and they informed me that we were going to start moving at 8 a.m. the following morning. The whale-watching location wasn't near, as we were meant to arrive the following morning. We were going to spend most of the day in the area, then move before sunset to arrive on the evening of the third day. The yacht was massive and had plenty of fully equipped rooms; it looked like it belonged to some wealthy business owners. Deborah informed me that one of their friends owned the yacht and that the tour was his present to them for their fortieth anniversary.

As soon as the yacht started moving, I began to search for Ziad, hoping to catch him before the trip went off. The captain mentioned that the area we were heading to wasn't that famous as it was mainly known by experts; that's why it wasn't visited by a lot of tourists. Travel agencies usually preferred whale-watching destinations that were closer to the island, "Whales don't get here before July, so we're going to their places. They're usually much calmer in that faraway area, so swimming with them is easier."

I spent that morning enjoying the trip with everyone. Every once in a while, I would have a glance at the ocean in hopes of spotting Ziad swimming nearby. A dolphin pod swam by, but he wasn't among them. I knew that because none of them tried to approach our yacht; they just swam away while racing each other and diving. During the evening twilight, as the radiating sunrays were reflected on the surface of the tranquil water, Ziad finally showed up. He emerged from the reflected sun rays above the ocean, breaking that charming image and overtaking it with his strong, twirling body. Unable to contain my happiness, I began to cheer enthusiastically in a way that surprised Deborah, who stood next to me. "That's Ziad, that's my dolphin!" I told her. A mix of delight and surprise took over her face, "I didn't think he was going to follow you. Seems like everything you said about him was true." "Do I talk about him that often?" I asked. She chuckled and said, "Like a little girl who shows off her new pet cat all day."

I wondered when he would grow weary of chasing the yacht, as he spent the whole day swimming and jumping around it. William told me, "Dolphins can swim all day long. Don't worry, he'll remain behind us. Plus, we'll stop in a bit so we can swim before nighttime." The yacht soon stopped and we had the chance to enjoy the water for around an hour, most of which I spent with Ziad. Our interaction was a source of surprise among everyone; it led the captain of the yacht to suggest that I set up a dolphin training center and he even offered to become my partner since I was a natural expert. Deborah wondered if she could try swimming with Ziad, so I asked him as if I was talking to a friend, and he didn't disappoint. Not only did he swim with her while she held on to him, but he also dove and danced with her the way we did together.

By nighttime, Ziad had vanished in the water. I assumed he was running a little late or that he was swimming underneath the surface and was going to appear at any time. Perhaps he was giving me the chance to rest. After I had dinner with the group, I decided to go to sleep. Shortly after, I randomly woke up because I had a dry throat, so I drank from a water bottle and tried to get back to sleep, but failed. I walked to the yacht's upper deck after putting on my life jacket, as we were always instructed to do.

I stood there and observed the large, mysterious ocean with its waves that were beginning to become a little higher, subtly moving the yacht from side to side. I was leaning against the fence of the yacht and examining the water's depth when I suddenly drowned in my thoughts. I remembered Kamel, but in a different way. I noticed how I didn't think about him for three whole days. I didn't think about his betrayal or the perfect picture he once created then shattered to reveal an indescribable ugliness beneath it. I had become healed by the beautiful nature, the greenery surrounding me everywhere, even at the top of mountains, the fulfilling breeze that carried the scent of coconuts, ocean water, and tropical forests. I had become healed by a sweet, cheery, friendly dolphin that I happened to call Ziad.

In the middle of my contemplations, I suddenly thought I spotted something moving behind the yacht. I assumed that Ziad was back, so I leaned forward with my body while strong grabbing the yacht's fence to look for him. I bent even more forward when I heard something splash against the water. "It must be him, he must be jumping to keep track with us." I'm not sure what happened after that, but the next thing I felt was my body jumping up and flying in the air then aggressively slamming against the ocean's water in a way that caused me immense physical pain, almost knocking me down.

I shrieked as loudly as I could, asking for help and begging the captain of the yacht to return for me, but no one seemed to hear me. I screamed Ziad's name, which was a desperate call that was done in hopes that dolphins rescued drowning people. The water was extremely cold, so I tried to beat my coldness with some hopeless body movements, but I was soon overwhelmed with pain. I stopped moving, letting myself flow with the help of my lifejacket. During the first couple of minutes, I assumed they were going to realize I fell and return for me, but a long time had passed without anything appearing on the horizon, not a yacht or even a random piece of wood.

I called out for Ziad one more time, but he didn't respond, and it soon became apparent I was only imagining that he was chasing the boat and that he was never around in the first place. I realized that I fell out of stupidity and gullibility, so I had to accept whatever was about to happen. Weeping in fear, I prayed to God, I promised I wasn't going to complain about my life and that I was going to cherish all the blessings I didn't pay attention to. I tried to recall all the prayers I knew and the ones I heard, so I could repent every sin I had committed or thought about committing.

"Dear God, I never hurt anyone in my life, so please help me get out of this!" I invoked, then I remembered that I did cause harm to many of my employees when I made harsh or unfair decisions against them, but it was an occupational hazard, I had to do it for the company's policy. I was at the forefront, which meant I had to penalize any employee for any mistake no matter how simple it was. "I promise that if I get out of this, I will change, I will help them out. I will do my best to never be unfair to anyone. Maybe I'll quit my job altogether and live with my parents until I get married, or maybe I'll just live with them forever."

The cold was beginning to move from my skin to my bones, then it sneaked all the way to my organs and my brain, which made me shiver, unable to speak or even think. I cried again, "Oh God." I took a deep breath to be able to continue praying, "You're my … only savior and the most m-m-merciful." I didn't finish the sentence as my teeth chattered. It felt like the end, but it was painful to know it was happening that way. A slow, cold, painful death. A coldness that crawled up on me and choked me slowly. My vision was gone and I started to feel my spirit withdrawing quietly out of my body.

ZIAD—MOTO MUAYA, APRIL 2019

I no longer paid much attention to the possibility that Arwa might be the woman meant to accompany me to the island so that my transformation of becoming a "rare" human would be complete. Her mere company was enough to make me happy. Spending time with her was much more significant than any other privilege I might gain later; her presence in my life on its own was enough privilege for me. If that was how humans defined love, then I loved her.

The day she intended to head to the whale-watching area was the same day I was supposed to go to the island, but I decided to postpone my visit that time. Nothing was going to happen to the island if I visited it one day later, but if I had missed a day with Arwa, that would be a different story. I knew her days here were limited, and after those days, she was going to travel to where I wasn't ever going to find her again.

I set out towards the area where humpback whales usually swim during that time of the year. It was a remote destination that would take an entire day of swimming to reach. I decided to surpass Arwa's yacht then rest for a bit so we could meet halfway, but it was an unwise decision. I lost their yacht, and it took me a large portion of my time and energy to find it. I proceeded to use my echolocation in an attempt to locate all boats that had a size suitable for that kind of trip. Luckily, there weren't many boats in the area, so I was able to find Arwa's yacht.

When she saw me, Arwa cheered so joyfully that she almost fell off the yacht with enthusiasm. I learned that humans think all dolphins look the same, that's why I was nervous she might not recognize me, but she proved me wrong. She seemed to be certain that the dolphin swimming in her direction was certainly Ziad, even though I was swimming far away from her. I jumped multiple times so I could get to her faster while trying to contemplate her in every jump. I thought she was "pretty," as humans say, but I didn't understand their beauty standards except for the theoretical explanations that my mind grasped while being on the island. I didn't even understand why the concept of "beauty" mattered that much to them.

What difference does it make if a person is "beautiful" according to those standards or not? Do men feel happy with a woman if she's physically beautiful but unhappy the other way around? Does beauty provide any sort of privilege to its owner that is not extended to those who lack it? I didn't feel happy with Arwa because she had a tiny nose and wide eyes and a slim figure; I felt that happy because I enjoyed her inner genuine being, I was attracted to the identity behind those features, and my feeling wasn't going to be any different if her nose was bigger. That didn't matter anymore! She was going away soon anyway, leaving me with a memory as delicate as her laugh.

The yacht finally stopped and Arwa greeted me the way a child does when he finally sees his parents after a long day of being separated from them. We spent a lovely time together, a time I added to the list of extremely magical moments in my memory. When she asked me to swim with her old friend, it was an unforgettable experience for me, only because she kept watching me with joy and pride.

By nighttime, she disappeared inside the yacht, so I decided to sleep till sunrise and rely on the water current to move in the direction of her yacht. After that, I could catch up with them again by using my full speed. The right half of my brain fell asleep when I suddenly heard a faint sound that whispered "Ziad" reaching me from afar. My brain became completely alert to those remote cries for help, and I soon distinguished that they belonged to Arwa. I worried about what might have happened to her as I rushed out towards the voice. It eventually, however, stopped, which terrified me even more.

While searching for her, my focus was scattered due to sleep deprivation and my excessive worry over her. Was it possible that she fell off the yacht? That question kept repeating inside my head while I proceeded to look for her using echolocation, but to no avail. I decided to swim in the direction of her yacht, then emitted my sound waves again. Overwhelmed with panic and fear, I spent a long time desperately looking for her, until her voice finally reached me again as she prayed, "Please God." I was luckily able to determine the direction from which her words were uttered, and I emitted my sound waves in that direction till I was finally able to locate where she was.

I swam like I was trying to escape a large flock of violent orcas, jumping in the air consecutively and splashing my fluke against the water as hard as I could, until I finally reached Arwa. She was either sleeping or unconscious; I couldn't determine at first. I tried to give her a shake but to no avail. Her heartbeats were slow and quiet, so I immediately realized her life was in danger and that I had to do something about it instantly. I knew I had to get her out of the water, as I had learned that the reason most humans die in oceans is due to their body temperature going down. The nearest island was an hour away, so I had to start swimming as soon as I could.

I grasped her lifejacket with my mouth and pushed her in front of me, then set out to swim as fast as I could in that tricky position. The waves were challenging, but I didn't lose hope. Yes, I truly did love her, at least the way humans perceive love. That meant I had already achieved one of the required conditions that were going to provide me with the rare ability to transform into a human on any land. On my way to the nearest island, my head started to consider the possibility of heading south instead of north; in the direction of my magical island. If I threw us both in the whirlpool that takes me to the island, I was going to spend a long time alone with Arwa. If I followed that plan, however, it would put her life in more serious danger. Her pulse was getting weaker and she wasn't going to endure that long journey in the cold water. No, I wasn't going to risk her life or sacrifice it to achieve a wild possibility that may or may not happen.

Even if her life wasn't in danger, who was I to decide her life for her and drag her to a strange place away from the rest of humanity. To hell with that island and its impossible rules: To save her from death and love her at the same time! But how could I be sure I love a woman if I risk her life for a purpose that only serves me and not her? "Shut up, Ziad! Just save Arwa and go after your dream some other time, or give up on those silly dreams altogether," I spoke to myself decisively, putting an end to my hesitance and fighting that selfish thought of taking her to the magical island. I carried on swimming when I suddenly heard her whimper "Ziad!" She was calling out my name in the peak of pain while I greedily considered risking her life for my own benefit. Her voice pushed me to continue swimming even faster. I exerted all the power, strength, and energy left in my body so I could take her to the nearest safe zone; perhaps someone out there could rescue her. The least I could do was get her out of the water so she could regain her normal body temperature.

The waves became even higher, violently hitting me as I went my way. They struck from both directions at the same time, when we were suddenly swallowed in a random whirlpool that appeared out of nowhere. I kept spinning inside it while desperately trying to hold on to Arwa. I was pressing on her lifejacket with my jaw as hard as I could so I wouldn't lose her in the whirlpool when we were suddenly thrown outside of it, where I found myself at the shore of Moto Muaya, the magical island.

I didn't question that strange incident for too long, I was only concerned with saving Arwa's life. I went out to the shore in my human form, dragging her until we were both far away from the water. I walked to the trees and brought some dry branches, then returned to her and created a fire. It wasn't strong enough, as her body's temperature was extremely low, so I left again to bring extra wood. I got a small number and returned to her, adding to the fire, then set out one last time and returned with the last batch, eventually creating enough heat to warm her up.

I finally broke down and fell asleep right next to her, where I saw the three elderly ladies in my dream. It was nighttime and they were sitting in their cave, with some fire source lighting up the entrance. I asked them, "How did we get here? I wanted to take her to the nearest land and save her," to which the elderly lady replied, "Because you chose her over yourself, Ziad. That's the biggest proof of your love." "You're misinterpreting it, I just wanted to do the right thing. Even if I did love her, there are still other conditions that have to be applied. Who said Arwa loves me back? And how do you know that she's feeling sorrow and pain?" "We don't know yet, it's your duty to find out yourself whether the rest of the rules apply or not. You will keep her here with you for a week." I yelled angrily, "No, I want to return her to where she belongs. I don't want her to suffer for my sake." The old woman chuckled sarcastically and said, "We know you wish you could keep her in the island for a week. Remember, you don't know where this woman belongs, even if she was born somewhere far away from here and lived her whole life there, many humans live where they don't belong. What if that particular person belongs here with you?"

ARWA—MOTO MUAYA, MAY 2019

I opened my eyes with difficulty while trying to cover them from the sun's rays with my hand. I felt confused and dissociated as I tried to remember what had happened to me. The last thing I remember was shivering from the extreme coldness of the ocean and finally passing out before I felt some sort of physical force shake me. After that, I heard a dolphin's sound; it was certainly Ziad's! I believe I dozed off, then regained consciousness multiple times, the last of which was when I was spinning inside a tornado or a whirlpool of some sort, but I didn't even panic due to how powerless I felt.

I looked around and noticed plenty of ashes and burning wood next to me. I then looked out to the ocean and noticed how its calm waves gently touched the black-sanded beach. As soon as I saw a stranger sleeping near me, I suddenly regained my full awareness and became completely alert. I wasn't sure if he was just sleeping or fully unconscious. I approached, then contemplated him: he was dark-skinned, like one of the native inhabitants, with high cheekbones, narrow eyes, soft hair, and strong muscles. He wore a skin-tight grey leather suit; it was short-sleeved so it revealed his forearms but concealed his legs down to his mid-calves.

Suddenly, he woke up. When he saw me standing next to him, he started to appear nervous. "Arwa! When did you get up?" he exclaimed. I was shocked to hear him speak in Arabic, so I asked, "Who are you? And how do you know who I am?" He fidgeted nervously as if I had just asked him about an undercover mission, then he spoke while stuttering, "I'm a fisherman, I live with my parents on Muaya's island. My boat was shattered by the same tornado that brought you here." I raised my left eyebrow questioningly, waiting for him to finish his story. "I arrived here right before dawn. After that, I saw a dolphin throwing you out on the shore, so I took you as fast as I could and started a fire to keep you warm. Your temperature was extremely low."

Ziad truly did save my life; that meant I wasn't hallucinating before. The man who stood before me, however, defending himself in front of my accusing questions, continued Ziad's mission and saved my life. I felt grateful to him and his wondrous favor, but my curiosity beat my gratitude so I asked again, "How do you know my name? And how do you speak Arabic?" to which he answered, "You said your name when you were hallucinating during sleeping, and as for my Arabic ... that's a long story." The fact that he spoke classical Arabic and not any other Arabic dialect was particularly interesting.

I then realized I hadn't asked any of the more important questions, like where I was and how I was going to head back to Bora Bora. The stranger said, "We're on an uninhabited island, so our only hope is that some boat or yacht comes by and saves us." My eyes widened in shock and I said, "What if nothing shows up?" "We're not going to wait forever, of course. I will start making a small raft that takes us to the nearest island. I am an expert in the area, so don't worry." I didn't like his suggestion, so I muttered something to myself about waiting for Ziad, the dolphin that saved my life, to come back and get me out of there. The stranger disapproved and said, "That's insane, a dolphin can't travel in water with you." so I replied speaking in classical Arabic, mimicking him, "He's smarter than most humans and we have a bond that you can't understand."

He shrugged and asked me, "Are you hungry?" His question infuriated me! Why would I concern myself with food or hunger when I was lost on a deserted island with nothing but the company of a stranger who didn't know how to get me back. I wondered if everyone was looking for me and how my parents were going to react to me not responding to their phone calls. Was Deborah going to find my phone and tell them I fell in the ocean? They would be overcome with fear. My father would pay for a ticket that cost a fortune just to travel for thousands of kilometers and look for me. His search wasn't going to matter, but it's his paternal sentiment that always made him try to surround me with safety since I was a little girl.

"What's your name?" I asked him, then I realized I was speaking in Egyptian Arabic, and repeated the same question in classical Arabic. "Do you prefer that I speak like that?" He smiled politely and said, "Yes, Classical Arabic is easier for me to understand." So, I said, "Well, what do you suggest we eat?" He offered to roam around the area and look for edible fruits in the trees. "Do you know the area well?" I asked him, to which he shook his head defensively, so I said, "Well, then we will ... hope for the best." I said the second half of the question in Egyptian, laughing as I walked by him.

We noticed a shrub that was no longer than two meters; it had large leaves that dangled down to the ground. He picked greenish-yellow fruits that were the size of an apple and had grainy surfaces. He claimed it was called a "breadfruit" then split it into two halves and gave me one. I tasted it hesitantly; its taste reminded me of a potato. We then continued searching among the trees as I prayed to find something more filling. Luckily, the island had pineapple, banana, and papaya trees in addition to a fruit that was called "noni," which was the size of a potato. It tasted somewhat bitter, but he mentioned it was nutritious. He said I had to eat one per day for as long as we stayed on the island. During our walk, he filled a waterskin bag he had with water from a nearby stream and we drank from it, then he filled it with another round.

On our way back, he recounted the story of how he learned to speak Arabic after I kept insisting. He told me how his father used to work as a driver in Saudi Arabia when he was a kid and that he started learning Arabic there, then he continued to learn Arabic after they returned. "Why would your dad work in Saudi Arabia? You're French at the end of the day!" He nodded in agreement and clarified that a Saudi man who once joined a fishing trip in Bora Bora admired his father's work, so he offered him a job in a fishing company that he owned there. It was a strange story that had many plot holes, but I chose to believe it anyway. We sat on the shore, where I sat near the water whereas he chose to sit away from it. I wished Ziad would show up at that moment, emitting his musical whistles and showing off his dances, then take me back with him to Bora Bora. I yelled out loud, "Ziad, Ziad!" but there was no response. "Do you really think he's going to hear you? And why the name Ziad anyway?" the stranger asked me. "It's the name I chose for him. And yes, I'm sure he'll return for me."

I returned to the shore, after I grew weary of calling out for Ziad, and sat on the sand with the stranger for some time. I eventually got bored, so I proceeded to build a sandcastle to try and kill time. The stranger asked for permission to help me build it, which I didn't mind. I asked for his name, to which he answered that it was "Mawry." "Nice to meet you, Mawry," I said. He tried to continue building the outer fence of the castle that I had forgotten to build at the beginning. He then excused himself, headed towards the trees, and returned with a group of dry branches, which he proceeded to break into smaller pieces. He used them as supporting tools for the castle, adding an impressive look to the construction. I kept bringing more water to carve the sand while he brought more wood branches. Eventually, half the morning went by in the blink of an eye.

During that time, both of our eyes were fixated on the ocean, as we waited for any boat to pass by, while I silently searched for Ziad. Unexpectedly, I felt safe and reassured that I was going to return home within a short amount of time. I felt that a lifeboat was going to show up at any given moment. We no longer live in a day or age where people vanish on deserted islands. I was also certain of William and Deborah's love and care for me, they were undoubtedly searching for me. Even if no one was looking for me, it seemed like "Mawry" was an expert on the ocean and could save us. I had decided before I got on the plane that I was going to let go of all my fears and doubts so I would be able to enjoy every moment. That's why after having spent the first hour on the island in fear and anticipation, I decided to let everything flow naturally and try to enjoy my time there.

In the middle of the day, he suggested hunting a rabbit and then grilling it, which I thought was a great idea. "Let's grill some of that breadfruit and eat it with the rabbit, it's going to taste exactly like grilled potatoes," I said, then I asked him to create a fire for me before he went hunting. He enthusiastically agreed, so we picked many dry branches before he made a fire, then vanished among the trees. Minutes after he disappeared, I suddenly heard the sound of a beloved whistling coming from the direction of the water. I looked towards its direction and found Ziad jumping in the water, repeating his whistling as if he was inviting me to get in the water and share a quick dance with him.

ZIAD—MOTO MUAYA, MAY 2019

After I started a fire for Arwa, I left her and hurried off to the trees, heading towards the rocky shore so I could jump in the ocean and return to my original image, the one she was longing to see. It was striking how differently I felt after I interacted with her in my human form. My eyes caught things I didn't notice before as a dolphin; even the simple touch of our hands created an intimacy that drastically exceeded the warmth I felt when she fully attached herself to my dolphin body. It was a strange feeling that made me wonder how I would feel if our human bodies touched.

I was too scared to confront her with the truth; I didn't understand why. Maybe I knew how much it would shock her or how she would have a hard time comprehending it in the first place. I was afraid her feelings towards me, which I was yet to determine, might change. She could potentially perceive me as a black magic practitioner or demonically possessed or any of those myths that humans believe in. I preferred to let her know who I was as a human, and if she happened to fall in love with me, then I would reveal the truth to her. If not, I would simply help her get back without telling her who I was; it would be enough for me to let someone like her genuinely know my real, honest self that way.

When I went back to being a dolphin and swam near the shore close to where she was sitting, I instantly caught joy in her eyes, the same kind I saw every time we met. That time, however, there was an additional sentiment besides the joy that I didn't understand. She got into the water and swam until she reached me. Of course, I didn't dare approach the shore so I wouldn't risk getting pushed by the waves to the island, where my upper half would transform into a human's body and my lower half would stay in its dolphin form. That would cause irreversible trauma to her.

I spent around an hour with her, during which we performed the water dance that we had perfected. We swam round and round, jumped and spun together in the air. Every once in a while, she swam back to the shore to check if Mawry, the human version of myself, had returned with the rabbit. When we were taking a break together in the water, she murmured, "I wish I could have some fish, that Mawry guy looks like he doesn't know how to hunt." She used her Egyptian dialect when she addressed me as a dolphin, and classical Arabic when she talked to me as a fellow human, which didn't make sense. Obviously, there was no reason a dolphin would understand her dialect more than an Arabic-speaking human would. Maybe she believed her dolphin understood her regardless of how she talked or what her words meant in the first place.

I swam away from her and headed to an area that was filled with flocks of fish, then returned with one in my mouth. She held it in her hand, walked to the beach, and put it next to where she was sitting, and by the time she had returned to the water, I brought her another fish. Following that pattern, I brought her six fish. When she returned to me after the last fish, I simply rubbed my head on her hand and turned around as if I was saying goodbye to her, then I dove into the water. I heard her say, "Don't be late tomorrow." It seemed obvious that she accepted my role as Ziad the dolphin, and that she realized that it was impossible or at least dangerous for a dolphin to take her from the island and travel with her for thousands of miles to another island.

Returning to the island through the rocky shore was a much more difficult task. I had to get in the water and surf a wave that was about to hit me, which made me fly high up in the air before I fell on the rocks, returning to my human form. I could feel bruises and overall strong physical pain from hitting those rocks. I decided to search for a rabbit to hunt for Arwa so I could justify my long time away. I searched among the trees for some time, but to no avail. I didn't search between the mountains or by the stream, even though the possibility of finding a rabbit there was better, but I simply felt a strong desire to return to Arwa. I did, however, pick some fruits on my way back to her.

When I finally arrived at where she had been waiting for me, I pretended to look shocked when I saw her grilling the fish. "Where did you get this from?" "Ziad was here." "Ziad, the dolphin? Where did he go?" I asked, to which she said boastfully, "He came and played with me for some time and brought me fish as soon as I told him I wanted to have some." She then spaced out for a while before saying, "I don't remember when was the last time anyone truly cared that much for what I want." She then looked somewhat uncomfortable, as if she said something she shouldn't have, then she added jokingly, "Looks like you're a bad hunter." "I found a rabbit but it ran away from me, so I picked those fruits for you." She laughed and said, "In Egypt, we have a saying that goes, "Crows only can bring the most disappointing gifts," then continued to laugh.

She tasted the first fish to make sure it was fully cooked, chewing it quickly while concentration took over her face. She then signaled to me that it was ready to be eaten and invited me to join her. We proceeded to dip pieces of fish in the breadfruit that she also grilled, before she suddenly said, "We're just missing some salt." Then, as if she remembered something, she said, "You could bring us a hollow rock, then we could pour some ocean water in it and boil it until the water evaporates and leaves the salt at the bottom." "Okay! I'll do that after we're done eating." We finished our fish, then she headed towards the water, where she washed her hands for a long time. I wiped up my hands using sand and tree leaves, then left her and walked towards the forest. She asked, "Aren't you going to wash your hands?" "I'll wash them in the stream and get us some water, then I'll look for the hollow rock," I said.

I didn't wait for her response and walked away quickly. It occurred to me to head to the elderly ladies' cave and ask them to lend me a stone vessel. When I reached the cave, they welcomed me in an unusual manner. The one sitting in the middle said, "There are two vessels behind that branch, take them and take that waterskin with you too." I was taken aback, but before I could ask how they found out I needed those things, she said, "The island tells us everything. It also told us that Arwa doesn't apply to its conditions." I froze in my place and breathed in deeply, "Huh? How did the island know that?" She said strictly, "The island knows everything about anyone who steps foot on it." I said furiously, "Then why did it bring her here? I wanted to return her to a nearby island, but Moto Muaya decided to bring her." The elderly woman then told me that Arwa didn't go through the overwhelming sorrow that the island required as a rule and that her experience wasn't painful enough: her husband cheated on her and that's all that there was. I exclaimed, "Isn't love a big deal for humans? And isn't losing it one of the greatest causes of pain and grief?" In response she said, "She didn't care that deeply for him. Yes, she loved and trusted him, but her experience didn't shatter her soul, it didn't take out a part of her heart and throw it in burning flames. Arwa lost a love that went on for less than a year and it didn't force her to make an irreversible compromise. You will need to look for someone else, Ziad." "Ziad?" I asked, surprised. "Isn't that the name that Arwa calls you?" she said.

I decided to ignore her and go back to the main issue: the great sorrow that the island required! I wanted to protest and ask the island to make an exception, I wanted to say that she was unhappy and that was enough, that her whole being didn't have to be shattered in pieces so she could fit in their rules. However, I simply took the vessels and walked back, feeling frustrated and defeated. I was beginning to get more captivated by her love like she was a part of me. I knew she loved Ziad the dolphin and liked Mawry the human, which meant she was going to soon love me in both of my forms. Humans fall in love quickly and things rapidly evolve when it comes to them, then they make love the center of their lives and connect their entire happiness to it. I knew she was going to be happy as soon as she learned that I was one soul, but existed in two different entities for her.

Nothing mattered anyway at that point! I walked slowly, repeating those words to myself and wondering why I was that upset to hear their news. Less than a day ago, I was telling myself I wanted to return her to her old life wherever it was meant to be and simply settle for the time I spent with her. Was I affected that much by the news, or did I desperately want to receive my reward? Was I only looking forward to enjoying my humanity on any land, at any time I chose, and living among other humans while still being allowed to return to my life whenever I wanted? No! What bothered me was how the elderly ladies appeared in my dreams and convinced me that I genuinely loved Arwa and that she could potentially be my other half, the one that could complete my existence. Did they visit me in my dream or was it a creation of my own brain? Was it a figment of wishes that my subconscious mind longed for and expressed in the form of a dream that included the elderly ladies, to add to its credibility?

When I finally arrived, the sun was about to set. Arwa had cleaned the space after she had gotten rid of the leftovers of our food and the ashes of the fire. A smile lit up her face when she saw me carrying the vessels, and she asked where I got them from. "I found them in a cave near the mountain," I said, to which she responded, "That means there are other people on the island." I waved my arm in disagreement, "No, of course not! They must have belonged to people that were here a while ago then left." She pouted her lips and said enviously, "Lucky people! A boat must have come and rescued them."

I told her that they must have done it without anyone's help, that they built a raft, like the one I intended to build. She said, "Let's begin working on it tomorrow just in case." I nodded in agreement and began to gather wood to create a fire that would keep us warm at night. Before I started moving, she asked me how we were going to sleep in the middle of nowhere and if it was safe in the first place. When I tried to reassure her, she said, "I'm not sure I can sleep like that." I suggested to try and sleep in one of the caves or under thick bushes, but she firmly disagreed. "No, we have to remain near the shore all the time in case anyone or anything passes by."

ARWA—MOTO MUAYA, MAY 2019

"There's something undeniably strange about that guy. It's something I can sense, but can't put into words. It isn't anything suspicious that creates discomfort, as much as it draws you in and sparks a sense of curiosity and fondness in you," I thought to myself as I watched Mawry walk away, heading towards the trees. Before that, he had started a fire for me and then told me he was going to fetch some fruits and return. Our first day spent together was comfortable. I still felt like I was stuck in a dream or some sort of elaborate hoax that was going to come to an end eventually, even though everything else indicated it was solid reality. My brain, however, was refusing to deal with the situation as seriously as it should have.

My favorite part about that day was Ziad showing up in the ocean. I admired that creature so much that I wished there was some kind of way I could bring him home with me. I wondered if he could somehow migrate to the Red Sea, where I could meet him in a place like

Ain Sokhna[23], even if I had to rent an apartment there and visit it once every week. The scenario took over my head, so I began to think about how he could travel, how I could explain the idea to him, and if I could even describe the geographical location in the first place. I began to compare the different tourist villages I knew in Sokhna and consider which ones were better: The ones situated on Suez Road or the ones by Zafarana Road?

I contemplated the possibility of swimming with Ziad on the beach of Stella de Marie or Porto Sokhna[24] and enjoyed the idea of spectators watching us in amusement. I pictured the looks of astonishment, mixed with envy, that would take over their faces. During the peak of those unrealistic fantasies whirling in my head, I saw Mawry heading towards me with a big pile of large, leafy branches over his shoulders. I ran to him and helped him put them down. When I asked why he brought them, he said, "You shouldn't be sleeping in the open air, especially since we're surrounded by trees."

I instantly admired his decency and politeness. I already knew the natives of the surrounding islands were nice and hospitable folks, like people who live in the countryside of Egypt, but I didn't expect Mawry to be that thoughtful and generous. Perhaps he only wanted me to like him! At the end of the day, he and I were alone together on a deserted island, so like any other man, he might have been only concerned about impressing me. I immediately shook off those thoughts and tried to dis-

---

[23] A town in Suez Governorate, in Egypt. It is famous for its tourist resorts and villages.

[24] Tourist hotels or resorts in Ain Sokhna that overlook the red sea

tract myself by helping Mawry build a small hut, one that was exactly my size. At first, he inserted four long branches in the soil, all of which were tilted towards the center of the construction. After that, he bound them together using smaller branches. I helped him stabilize the branches until we were able to build the right and left sides of the walls, but we still had the front and back ones left.

I joined him in fetching more branches so we could add another layer to my hut and make it wind-resistant. The length of the base was two and a half meters, the width was around a meter and a half, whereas the height exactly reached the top of my head. The dimensions of the ceiling were almost half the base dimensions, making it look like an imperfect cone. After we were finally done building it together, I told Mawry, "Now, let's make one for you," but he politely refused and said, "I don't mind sleeping in the open air. Plus, I think you've already exerted a lot of effort today." I still insisted on helping him build one, as I didn't want to owe anyone a favor, even if it was to a harmless, gentle, and well-mannered young man like Mawry. I thought that if I agreed to let him sleep in the open air while I slept safely inside my hut, it would be equivalent to allowing a stranger to pay for my bill in a café or restaurant. He tried to refuse again, but I threatened him that I was going to enter the forest by myself and search for the proper branches, which would be dangerous of course, so he had to comply with my request. I didn't mean what I'd said, nothing was worth walking alone in a forest, but he luckily went with it anyway.

We spent almost the same amount of time building Mawry's hut. I nearly fell to the ground when I was trying to balance one of the branches and ended up in a strange position, so I burst out laughing as I tried to get myself back up. Mawry smiled awkwardly as if he wasn't sure what to do, or whether he should be helping me, holding me, or holding on to the branch. It appeared like he was constantly trying his best to not cross any line or invade my personal space in any way. Even though I had become apprehensive and cautious towards most men, I found myself naturally getting used to Mawry, as I experienced a sense of familiarity towards him, especially as we built those huts together.

When we were done with his hut, I finally entered my tiny new sanctuary. I stretched my body out on the black sands and instantly fell asleep; it was a deep and dreamless sleep. I didn't even experience the usual shortness of breath I had in my sleep that was caused by my chronic sinusitis. It seemed as if the clean ocean breeze had magically healed me, making my sleep calmer without resorting to any medications. The following morning, I woke up and saw Mawry, who had gotten up before me, sitting on the ground and trying to start a fire. He had four fish by his side, one of which was still alive and struggling to find its way back to the water. He also had a ceramic vessel next to him that he had brought to extract the salt and use it for our food, as I had requested before. Moreover, he had some breadfruits by the fire. I asked, "How did you get the fish?" "I just woke up and saw them by the shore, then a dolphin showed up and threw the last one at me. When I went to get it, he swam away immediately." I smiled happily and said, "It must be Ziad! He knows you can't fish, so he did it for me."

I didn't wait for Mawry to respond to my somewhat rude comment, as I immediately ran towards the ocean and called out Ziad's name multiple times, but I didn't receive a response. I then returned to Mawry and helped him grill the fish. After that, I heated the ceramic vessel that had been filled with water so I could extract the salt from it. I put it down, took my waterskin bag with me, and walked to the nearest water source. I was filling my bag with water as I contemplated a nearby mountain: there were plenty of thick shrubs by its foothill, whereas its peak was covered in greenery, like all the mountains in the area. On my way back, I feasted my eyes on the undeniable beauty of the island. I noticed some flowery trees, so I picked some of their scented flowers and brought them with me to put them in my hut and add a cozy touch to it.

After breakfast, Mawry told me he was going to gather some sharp rocks he could use for cutting down the trees that we were supposed to build our raft with, so I offered to join him. While we walked together, I began to tell him more about myself: the long journey that made me end up on that island, my job, and my busy life in Cairo. He told me about his loyalty and dedication to his home country, talking about France's collectivities and explaining how those islands were created by old volcanos, which explained why greenery covered every inch of them. The way he talked about his country reminded me of how poets write about their lovers.

"Your country is worth being adored. It carries an irresistible beauty," I told him, to which he said, "Your country is also magical in its way. The desert is just as beautiful as green lands." I said somewhat aggressively, "Egypt is more than just a desert." His face turned red and he immediately apologized for offending me. I laughed and said, "You're a nice guy, Mawry. And yes, you're right, Egypt's mostly a desert, but it has a lot of green spaces. Many roads connect between cities of Delta where the entire horizon is filled with greenery, despite those scattered bulks of cement." I then added, "It also has beautiful beaches where dolphins like Ziad sometimes show up, even though I doubt there's any other dolphin in the world like Ziad." Mawry's face was still red, maybe it had even become redder than before, as he said in surprise, "Really?" "Yes, Ziad understands me like no one ever has. He's intelligent and empathetic and would do anything for me, which is something I have never found in a human being."

We were able to gather many sharp, large rocks. Mawry found an additional coarse rock that he intended to use to sharpen the edges of the other rocks. We then headed to a spot that had thin-branched trees that could be easily broken down into pieces. I picked a tree and Mawry picked another, then we began to patiently and calmly cut them down. I could hear a group of hummingbirds hidden in different trees, but they weren't visible to me. After some time, I spotted a rabbit hopping nearby and looking around in apprehension. I hissed at Mawry so he could pay attention to me, then I discreetly pointed at the rabbit. Mawry subtly stood up, sneaked towards the rabbit, then jumped at it, trying to hunt it down, but the rabbit managed to hop away from him. I stood up, trying to prevent the rabbit from escaping, and threw myself at it, but it managed to get away once again. I burst out laughing while still trying to run after him, while Mawry tried to bombard him from the other side.

I didn't stop laughing for a second while we were attempting to hunt the rabbit down, whereas Mawry took the task quite seriously. We were finally able to catch it before we sat on the ground to catch our breaths. I was still laughing hysterically, but Mawry stared at me in surprise before he finally joined me in my laughing fit. He then asked, while trying to catch his breath, "Do you take everything so lightly?" "Of course not! But this isn't real life. Ever since I landed in Tahiti's airport, I decided to let go of everything I left back home. My problems, my responsibilities, and my continuous disappointment in life and the people in it. I wanted to revive my heart here, away from everything." Then I added, looking away from the rabbit that was being skinned, "Of course coming to this island is a separate experience. I dissociated from the whole world, even though I'm only on my second day."

I was telling the truth! I felt like my heart was being renewed in Tahiti and Bora Bora, but on the island, I felt like I was rebuilding my soul, with the help of a kind stranger and a dolphin that looked after me from afar. I wasn't sure, however, if that was truly how I felt, or if I was in an extreme state of denial regarding that overwhelming situation. It was a lot to deal with: ending up on an abandoned island and preparing for a terrifying ocean trip on a basic wooden raft, even if I was led by a sailor and a dolphin that was trying to keep me alive. Maybe it wasn't denial as much as it was a general underestimation of events. There was nothing to fear or do but to consider myself on a two-month vacation—maybe even a two-year vacation—from my normal life.

By the first half of the following day, Mawry and I had finished cutting down two trees before we started working on two more. I was getting more and more used to Mawry since we had been doing everything together and he rarely left my side. Ziad visited me whenever I would return to my hut by the ocean to take a break from cutting down trees. Meeting Ziad usually made me forget about my fatigue. I would get in the ocean and swim with him, then return to Mawry in the woods, where he would be dripping wet as he loved to go swimming in the stream. I would jokingly scold him for procrastinating, then we would get back to business.

I was able, without necessarily planning it, to make Mawry loosen up and have fun. I could tell he cared for me and was too careful not to offend me in any way. On the third day, I asked him to stay by the trees, continue cutting them down, and avoid going near the stream no matter what happened as I wanted to bathe in it. I needed to clean up, wash my clothes, and change my body odor. I took a handful of scented flowers with me, then began to take off my clothes there. I initially took off the outer layers and remained in shorts and a sleeveless shirt. I didn't dare take off my clothes completely even though I knew I was alone and Mawry wasn't going to show up.

I dipped my clothes in the water repeatedly and spread them on a tree branch that was well-exposed to the sun. I got in the stream, washed the naked, upper half of my body, rubbed it with the scented flowers, then repeatedly dipped myself in the water. After that, I threw my bra right at the spot that was heavily exposed to the sun so that it would dry as well. After that, I put my sleeveless undershirt on again and dove with my body in the spring.

I remained in the spring for a long time, enjoying the fresh water that flowed from a nearby water source and waiting for my clothes to dry. Eventually, I stood up and began moving to the other side of the stream, where I had spread out my clothes, but I was startled to see a large rat randomly appear out of nowhere. It came out of two rocks and ran quickly towards me, riding my arm so it could arrive on the opposite side. I shrieked in panic while struggling to jump out of the water. I stood and tried to quickly step up out of the spring before another, larger, rat jumped from the rocks. I screamed one more time before I slipped and fell, which made my head slam against the rocks, causing me to pass out.

ZIAD—MOTO MUAYA, MAY 2019

I heard Arwa shriek from afar, which made me want to go against her wish and hurry to the spring so I could check on her as fast as I could, but I froze. I told myself it could have been an insignificant squeal that I perceived to be more dangerous than it really was, so I could have an excuse to sneak a look at her. When she screamed again, I couldn't help but run towards the spring. I hadn't caught any wild animals or dangerous creatures on the island, but the possibilities were still endless. Perhaps the island was playing games with us.

I reached Arwa in no time. She was unconscious on the ground by the edge of the water source, where she lay completely still with her eyes shut and her head mildly bleeding. I felt somewhat reassured when I realized she was breathing regularly, but when I shook her body to wake her up, she only released a short moan but didn't open her eyes. I adjusted her body's position to make her more comfortable, then I brought some water and poured it over her head, but it didn't work. The wound was minor, but it continued to bleed. I left her and rushed to a nearby grassy area, one that grew herbs that were known for their healing effects, then I took out a batch and returned to Arwa. I rubbed the herbs in my hands and pressed them against the wound, which made her groan in pain. She finally opened her eyes.

The moment she noticed me standing in front of her, she blushed, crossed her arms against her chest protectively, then yelled, "Look the other way." I suddenly realized she was only wearing a tight, sleeveless, wet shirt that revealed most of her upper body. I turned the other way and shut my eyes tight, but the image of her body remained stuck in my head. I felt my heart race as soon as that picture of her wet body lying on the ground took over my brain. I felt embarrassed and uncomfortable, so I desperately attempted to get rid of those thoughts, as my eyes remained closed and my face directed towards the stream. She once again yelled, "Don't you dare look." Her threatening tone was further reinstating that picture in my head, moving something inside me that felt new and purely human. The way a man sees a woman is entirely different from anything I was used to my whole life as a dolphin. It was great enthusiasm mixed with guilt as if I had stolen something personal from her.

The constant popping of the image inside my head had revealed new details to me about Arwa. Moreover, I caught myself enjoying those details and not only visualizing them, which would increase the feeling of guilt. Whenever I would try to kick the image out of my head, it would only go away for a few seconds, then stubbornly return. That's when I would give in to it and its details all over again. "Now you can look," she spoke distantly. I said, "I'm sorry, I got scared when I heard you scream more than once. I didn't mean to—" I didn't find the proper words to complete my sentence. Was I supposed to say, "I didn't mean to be contemplating your beautiful body then keep that image to myself"? or "I didn't mean to keep summoning the image of your body over and over during those past short minutes and enjoy it every time it pops up?" She got up and started to walk as I followed her, "It's okay, Mawry! Thank you for saving me, and thank you for those foul-smelling herbs you used for my wounds." I replied, "But they're effective," so she said jokingly, "But you didn't find any coffee beans lying around?"

I felt lighter as soon as she began to loosen up and laugh about it, and we soon went back to our usual chatter as if nothing had happened. When we returned to the trees that we had been cutting, I told her to go and have a little break. She initially refused, claiming that she felt fine, but I insisted, as I took the sharp rock from her hand, "I'll continue by myself. You should go and rest." She smiled gratefully, "As you wish." She walked towards the shore, while I kept staring at her back. As soon as I felt those lustful feelings rush back, I turned my head the other way. I tried to empty my suppressed energy into cutting down the tree, as I could feel my body heat up and my head obsess over that damned image of her lying down, then the image of her walking away. I felt the need to physically connect with Arwa so that she could soothe the flame that lit up in my chest, or whatever it was called. I thought about it for a while then made my decision: I headed towards the rocky shore, jumped into the ocean, and returned to the sandy beach as Ziad the dolphin.

Arwa was inside her hut. I let out consecutive whistles and clicks until she got out. I proceeded to jump in the water, encouraging her to join me. I needed to feel her tight grasp around my body, which she always did whenever we dove or jumped together. She began to explain, using signals, that she couldn't get in the water. After some stubborn insistence on my side, she finally headed towards me but avoided wetting her head. She held me tightly and said, "My head is wounded, so we can't dive." I responded to her with soft, considerate whistles, but I couldn't stop myself, so I proceeded to swim in circles as she rode on my back. She chuckled but continued to warn me against going underneath the water. I dove slightly so she could hang on to me more tightly, which she did, but then she said, "We can't dive or play around too much, Ziad." I obeyed her, but I decided to grab the opportunity of her holding me and jumped slightly above the water. That instantly made her hold me even more tightly, yet she warned me for the third time. I stopped moving and whistled gently while rubbing myself against her, so she said, laughing, "You just love to play. Ugh, let's just do it. Let's dive."

I couldn't contain my happiness. Not only was I overjoyed that she agreed to dive with me, but that she did it despite her fear of getting hurt. When I was in my dolphin body, she perceived me as someone dear to her, maybe even as a lover who she would endure pain for. This idea made me accept only one dive and two jumps with her, in addition to a third jump during which I spun with her vertically in the air. Her grip during that last jump felt different from the ones before. I received it as a humanly embrace that sparked warm emotions and combined two intimate heartbeats.

I finally brought Arwa back to the shore, pulled myself together, then headed to the rocky beach so I could transform into my human shape and get back to work. After becoming a human again, I noticed the drastic difference between my state when I headed to the shore and my state after I returned. I had completely calmed down as if I fed some sort of inner desire that was taking over my entire being. I had gone back to cutting down the tree when Arwa suddenly showed up with a shy smile on her face. She wanted me to bring her more of the herbs that I had used on her wounds before, "Ziad insisted on diving in the water, so I messed up my wound and it bled a little," she said apologetically. I pretended to be shocked, "Ziad insisted! You talk about him as if he's a real person who puts down rules." She said, "He has every right to! He cares about me more than anyone else does, he even saved my life."

I felt both happy and shy at the same time, but I tried to hide my feelings regardless. We began to walk towards the grassy area when I asked her, "So how did you know he wanted to dive with you? Do you communicate that well with dolphins?" "No, I don't. I only communicate well with Ziad! I get him just like he gets me." We finally reached the area where the herbs were. I picked some, rubbed them between the palms of my hands, then gave them to her so she could place them on her wound. Arwa, however, leaned forward, directed her head at me, and pointed at her wound so I could apply the herbs on it myself. I placed the herbs on the wound and pressed on them with my right hand while placing my left hand on her shoulder. She whimpered in pain, so I patted her shoulder and apologized. She raised her head and looked at me, "Thank you!" She stood so close to me that I was able to whiff her breath. I stepped back shyly when I felt like we had gotten too close to one another, then we started to walk back to our trees.

Things remained the same for a couple of days. Nothing worth mentioning happened, except that I had gotten closer to Arwa as a human, especially since she was beginning to loosen up and treat me with more openness. I continued to explore my energy and yearning for her whenever I transformed to a dolphin, as I would elongate our swimming sessions as well as our dances in addition to the high air-jumps of course. I was somehow trying to fill my heart with her embrace that I could only experience in my dolphin form. Sometimes, she would hold me extra close, perhaps resorting to the help of a dolphin so she could protect herself from getting closer to the human.

Things between us were evolving every day, as if Mawry and Arwa have become a harmonious couple that have been together for years, despite the tension and nervousness that we shared. The nervousness somewhat decreased with time, but it would never vanish unless I was being Ziad. When I was in my human form, we would get physically close to one another on multiple occasions, such as when we cut down the trees, hunted rabbits, or cooked together. We even went to the water source, played around with the water, and fell to the ground laughing. I was entering her world, in my human shape, slowly but surely. I felt myself softly sneaking into her heart until I finally concluded that my human form was as dear to her as my dolphin form. Things were going smoothly, until that day she witnessed me transform firsthand.

ARWA—MOTO MUAYA, MAY 2019

I had spent six days on the forgotten island, as I had called it, without being able to catch a trace or shadow of a boat. I accepted the reality of having to continue building a raft that would help us get out of the island, even though I wasn't too confident in its ability to sail across the ocean. Mawry kept reassuring me that he knew how to build the perfect raft that could sail all the way to America if only he managed to find the right tools and supplies.

I was stirring in my sleep inside my hut, as various feelings and thoughts overtook me, preventing me from falling asleep. Every day, Mawry and I became closer, which would make the large differences between our two worlds smoothly dissolve. Gradually, we continued to evolve as a compatible pair that was completely disconnected from the real world. In addition, we shared emotionally charged moments that kept drawing me closer to him to the extent that I would get overwhelmed with the need to get physically closer to him as well.

I would usually handle those inner desires by resorting to an unexpected method, as I would look for any reason to leave him then head to the ocean and surrender to its water. I would call out for Ziad and somehow, he would show up in no time, as if he lived near the island. I would hold on to him and we would jump and spin in the air together, which would calm me down and fulfill me in a way that erased any previous needs or desires, especially those feelings towards Mawry. After that, I would return to him and continue working as if nothing had happened.

When I finally fell asleep that night, I had a strange dream. I dreamt I was walking alone on the island and began to climb that mountain that I always felt curious about. Before I could do it, I was interrupted by a familiar-looking old lady who asked me what I was doing. When I told her, she said, "Don't let Ziad cut the trees by himself." I brushed it off with a laugh and told myself she wasn't making any sense, then continued to climb the mountain till I reached the top. I found myself standing on a rocky ledge that overlooked the ocean, then I looked next to me and saw Mawry standing there as well, but he was about to jump. I tried to call out his name, but no sound came out of me. He jumped and fell into the ocean, where he completely vanished. I could feel my heart shatter in fear before I suddenly saw Ziad appear from the same spot that Mawry had jumped into.

I followed him and jumped in the ocean too, where I met Ziad. I asked him about Mawry, but he didn't respond. Instead, he began to swim towards the shore, then he got out of the water, where I saw him with my own eyes transition from being a dolphin to a human. In other words, he transformed from Ziad to Mawry. Strangely, I wasn't surprised to witness that transition, as if it was some sort of familiar ritual which consisted of me dancing with Ziad in his dolphin form, then getting out of the ocean with his human form. Mawry took me by the hand and entered the hut with me. He held me tightly and squeezed me in his arms before he gave me a long kiss. He was about to step back, but I pulled him in closer so he could keep kissing me for a longer time. The old lady interrupted us when she suddenly entered the hut and said, "There are more important things that need to be done first."

As soon as I woke up, which was shortly before sunrise, I instantly headed towards the mountain, still in a state of bewilderment. I wasn't sure whether my mind was playing games or if that dream meant something. It was a provoking dream and, for some reason, it felt highly unlikely that it was only a creation of my delirious state of mind. I had always believed that dreams were more than just inventions made by our subconscious minds; sometimes they carried messages from above or from our unreachable loved ones. When I reached the foothill of the mountain, I began to search for a starting point to climb from. When I finally found one and intended to start climbing, I was alarmed to hear an old lady's voice say my name out loud. I was even more shocked when I turned around and realized it was the same woman I had just had a dream about.

"I am the guard of the island," she introduced herself. "And yes, I just visited you in your dream, to inform you that Ziad is Mawry." I instantly made fun of her and accused her of rambling and speaking nonsense, "We don't live in a world of mermaids that transform into humans when they're on land," I said. The old lady laughed and said, "Every myth has an origin. For a very long time, some species of dolphins could transform into humans. Some, like Ziad, can only transition on this particular island, while others can transition on demand, in any land or ocean." I found her words too bizarre and shocking, so I decided to walk away and avoid climbing the mountain, which was a useless idea in the first place. I heard her say, "Just keep watching him and you'll know."

I returned to the beach. I considered "watching him" as the old lady told me to do, or maybe just asking him to get in the ocean in front of me. Maybe I could wait until Ziad showed up, then hide in my hut and scream as if I was in extreme danger, which would force him to get out of the water and transform in front of my eyes. I accused myself of being insane, before I asked myself, "What would I lose if I carried out a little experiment? There's nothing reasonable about my story with Ziad from the beginning. What exactly makes sense about a dolphin that understands Arabic and interacts with me in that unique way, that he could even rescue me from drowning? And what happened then? I found myself on a mysterious island with a young man that appeared out of nowhere. What kind of tornado would make us both end up in the same place? How does he know classical Arabic and not the Saudi dialect if that's where he lived? Was it even possible for a person to travel to the other side of the world only to work as a fisherman?"

I decided to carry out my plan. When I went to Mawry, who was cutting down trees, I let him know I was going to wait for Ziad by the shore and ask him to hunt some fish for us. I then hid inside my hut and proceeded to watch the area through a small opening. Soon, I heard Ziad's whistling and saw him jump in the water to notify me of his arrival. I waited, then suddenly let out a loud shriek from inside my hut, which made Ziad jump out of the water multiple consecutive times as if he was trying to find out what was happening. I screamed again and again until Ziad began to swim closer to the shore. I panicked and almost got out of my hut; I knew how a dolphin getting stranded out of the water could be extremely dangerous. Moreover, that whole transformation into a human thing could easily be nothing but gibberish.

I rushed out of the hut at the same moment that Ziad got out of the water. At that moment, I saw him physically transform right in front of my eyes. Shockingly, he indeed turned from a dolphin to a human, in what looked like a CGI scene from a sci-fi movie. I cried out while trying to convince myself that I was hallucinating and that none of it was real. Mawry ran towards me and instantly tried to calm me down. I was, however, in a genuine state of shock. I was shivering and could barely see anything but a blur. He proceeded to try and explain that none of that was his choice, that he only wanted to return me safely to Bora Bora. He kept clarifying how he didn't mean to bring me to the island. Gradually, I began to somewhat pull myself together and slowly accept what I had just witnessed, but my stomach was still in knots due to his deceit. Ziad and Mawry were one soul, and in both his forms, he loved and cared for me, but the way he elaborately concealed his lie made me doubt this love. He was trying to explain how terrified he was of how I would react when I realized the truth. Then he did something that infuriated me so much that it nearly made me want to throw a rock at his face.

He started crying! He teared up while trying to convince me with his story, which was a big mistake. Suddenly, it felt like it was Kamel, with all his lewdness and deceit, who stood there in front of me, defending his lies. There was no logic behind that feeling, I knew they were two entirely different situations, but the sight of seeing a grown man cry had become a symbol of deceit after my bitter experience with Kamel. I left him and headed to the forest, after warning him against following me. I sat by the spring, which was the first spot that witnessed my passionate feelings towards Mawry. It was that passion that led me to escape to the ocean's water, where I swam and attached myself to his alter ego. Without knowing, I was running away from him, to him.

I sat and contemplated the fresh water that ran from the fountain and flowed into the spring, as my brain remained motionless as a result of the intense shock. I tried to comprehend the situation I found myself in. My feelings towards that soul were unclear in both cases. Was I crazy to develop feelings for that odd creature or was I a normal person who had just gotten out of a breakup that made her throw herself at the first person, or creature, she came across? Perhaps our presence on the island at the same time was the reason this state of semi-romance was created in the first place. None of that mattered now! I simply wanted to return to Bora Bora, and since he brought me on the island in a supernatural way, he had to get me back in a supernatural way as well. None of that basic raft nonsense.

I walked to the mountain, where I ran into the old lady again. I wanted to ask her endless questions, but I didn't know exactly know where to start. My head was spinning and I longed to talk to someone. When I spotted her near the foothill of the mountain, she was walking towards me in slow, yet steady, steps that weren't exactly befitting her old wrinkled face, which indicated she was at least seventy. She began to recount Ziad's story from the start. She explained that for him to become a part of the rare species that could transform on demand and on any land, he had to search for a woman he could love, then bring her to the island. In addition, that woman had to reciprocate his feelings, and she had to have gone through an overwhelmingly sorrowful experience. "Even though he loved you, and even though it had become his dream to become one of those rare dolphins with that special ability, he didn't choose to seize the opportunity and bring you to the island when you were in danger. He prioritized your safety and chose to bring you to the nearest island, because he was deeply concerned for your life," the old lady told me.

"Are you trying to tell me he didn't bring me here on purpose?" I asked doubtingly, to which she said, "Why would I lie? I don't even have the ability to do it. Ziad loves you and he chose to save your life instead of risking it. You love him too, Arwa, much more than you ever loved Kamel. Your love for Kamel wasn't genuine, but it was a perfect opportunity for a seemingly perfect marriage, one that was ornamented with excessive romance, but it fell apart at the very first obstacle it encountered." I felt furious at her accusations and intrusion into my life. I said, "What a strange coincidence! Let me guess: you're about to say I'm the right woman for Ziad since I went through that great heartbreak." The old lady laughed and said, "You're not suffering from a great heartbreak, you just lost a marriage opportunity; a fascinating picture that shattered right in front of your eyes, which is a passing frustration that you will get over as soon as you meet the next faithful man that comes your way." Then she laughed again before she added, "If there's such a thing!" I spoke bitterly, "Who are you to judge my feelings and rate my sadness in the first place? And how did you know all of this?" "I know you more than you know yourself. Every human carries some feelings that he chooses to reveal to himself and he uses those feelings to justify his words and actions. But there is always another layer of subconscious feelings, ones that are too real and deep that you don't always reveal to yourself. As a human being, you find it easier to believe the easy version of reality that matches your convictions. For example, it is easier for you to believe that your sadness over Kamel is one that was caused by lost love, but you would strongly deny any passing thought that tells you how you're only sad that you missed an opportunity for a better life."

Her words were shocking, as she sounded like a psychologist that shocked you with facts even you didn't know about yourself. I asked her to stop talking and to return me to Bora Bora, so she said, "What about Ziad? Don't you want to make him happy and help him achieve his dream?" I thought to myself, "That woman is crazy. She wants me to fall in love with a dolphin! What next? Is she going to tell me something along the lines of "loving a faithful dolphin is better than loving an unfaithful husband?" So I replied, "Even if I do love him, which is unlikely, how do I grant him his wish if I'm not that sad woman that island says I have to be?" She replied, "We can make that happen." "How? Are you thinking about disfiguring my body or killing one of my family members?" I asked sarcastically. To that she answered, "No, but you can go through an experience that makes you taste unimaginable sadness! Your consciousness will experience a real occurrence during which you'll forget that you're Arwa. You will live as a different woman at a different time and place." I then said, trying to understand what she was saying, "Like a dream?" "Something like that, but you will feel like you have lived a whole life and you'll form real memories of it. You're going to cry real tears, experience true pain, and you will keep getting revisited by that pain as if you genuinely experienced it in real life."

What she was describing sounded perhaps even stranger than the idea of a dolphin transforming into a human. I said, "Well, I don't have to do any of that. I don't love him, and I won't hang my whole life on a legendary marriage. This isn't a children's fairytale. I just want to get married, have kids, and live a normal life." The old lady pouted her lips and said, "I'm talking about experiencing true love, the feeling itself, not the results of which." So I said determinedly, "You're contradicting yourself. You just said that I have to be in love before I embark upon that sorrowful experience, so how could I enter it if I'm not even sure about my love?" She said as she stared into my eyes, "Because agreeing to go through that experience is enough proof of your genuine love, no one willingly puts himself in such immense pain as an indication of their gratitude. Listen to me, Arwa, your love for Ziad, whether you believe in it or not, isn't just about finding a perfect marriage candidate. That kind of love changes your outlook on life, it pulls your heart out of your chest, revives it, then returns it to you as if it is an innocent child's heart. Don't make your decision right away. Stay by yourself in the forest for a day, away from him, and consider it. Then you can decide if you want to make that sacrifice for that virtuous creature that loves you in a way that doesn't even exist in your world. Make your decision, and in the event that you don't want to go through it, the island will return you to Bora Bora in no time."

30

ZIAD—MOTO MUAYA, MAY 2019

You don't fully grasp how much you love someone until you have deeply drowned in that love. Everything humans have written about love still couldn't manage to describe half the things I felt towards Arwa, even though I hadn't initially realized the full extent of my feelings. I didn't know how to define that enormous cluster of overwhelming emotions, until that moment that she stormed off after finding out my truth. She wasn't convinced by my reasons, so she left after giving me a look that read, "I don't know who you are anymore," then seemed to head to the mountain.

Funnily enough, I had immediately figured out she was setting some sort of trap for me when I heard her scream at the top of her lungs inside her hut earlier. After hearing her first shriek, I realized it was Arwa's voice, so I tried to understand what was going on by using echolocation. When I realized the sound was coming from inside her hut, I told myself she must have gotten injured, but it wasn't a cry for help, which is what you would expect when someone gets hurt. She was screaming as if she was facing some sort of danger. Despite having figured that out, I still couldn't risk her safety, so I immediately swam to the beach and willingly transformed in front of her. I knew she was bound to find out the truth at any moment, so I let things take their course. What I didn't expect, however, was the rage and accusations I had to face when I tried to defend myself.

When she walked away from me, I kept pondering what to do for nearly an hour. "Do I go and look for her? Is it true, what they say about women: that what they express is the complete opposite of what they want? Is it true they claim that they don't want your apology, but still wait at a nearby corner expecting one? Do they pretend they can't stand to hear a word from you, but secretly anticipate an act of kindness to make them feel better? Is any of this true? Most importantly, does it make any sort of sense, or is it another pointless myth that the island taught me?" I knew the island was supposed to teach me human wisdom, which included their long history and interactions with one another, so does that mean that a relationship between a man and a woman, with all its complexities and layers, is part of that wisdom? It is claimed that the relationship between the two sexes has triggered countless events, turns, and changes in the history of humans. For example, one war was caused by a shunned relationship between a man and a woman, another because a man raped a woman. No, I believe that those are disgraceful simplifications of much larger issues. I believe that the island taught me those stories to prepare me to love, care for, and maintain a relationship with a woman, so I could eventually achieve the most superior transformation.

After some time, I decided to get up and walk to the forest, where I was able to hunt a rabbit and grill it. I grilled some fruits with it, then I brought the entire meal with me and went to look for Arwa. I wasn't planning to apologize or ask for her forgiveness. I wasn't entirely sure how she was going to interpret this step of me approaching her, but I couldn't leave her alone, knowing that she hadn't eaten. I finally found her sitting by the spring, staring intently at the water as if she was trying to decipher some code. She frowned as soon as she noticed me, but she didn't say anything. I piled some large leaves on top of each other, then placed half the grilled rabbit and two grilled fruits above them before I walked away without speaking. I walked slowly, making sure I was within the realm of her eyesight, so I could give her a chance to call out my name, but she didn't.

As nighttime was nearing, I found a nearby spot by the spring, one that wasn't visible to Arwa, and I began to work on building her a new hut. I chose to build it against three large trees, which gave it more support and made my job easier. After I was done, I headed to the spring, where I expected her to be, but she was nowhere to be found. I immediately felt scared and called out for her, but I didn't receive a response. I began to search for her before I spotted her walking towards the spring in silence as if she meant not to respond to me. "Could she be waiting for an apology?" I asked myself, but I couldn't find an answer. I said, "I built you a new hut so you could sleep in it." "Why?" "I don't want you to sleep outside,"

I answered her. She repeated, "Why?" When I couldn't find a proper response, I simply pointed to where the hut was.

As soon as she saw it, she looked somewhat happy, but she managed to suppress it as if she didn't want to share that happiness with me. I didn't ask her whether she liked it or not and decided to leave her alone instead. As soon as I turned the other way, she asked again, "Why?"

"I don't know why. I can't let you sleep outside, and I can't pressure you to return to your hut by the water if you don't want to," I told her. I contemplated her face and realized she was tearing up. She asked with a softer voice, "But why?"

"I don't know. You're, you're—" I choked as I could feel the words get stuck in my throat. I didn't know what the rest of that sentence could be or what I was supposed to tell her in that situation, but she tried to encourage me to continue speaking, "I'm … what?"

"You're Arwa. You don't deserve to be taken for granted or left to struggle alone. You shouldn't be forced to do something you don't want, you're—" She got closer to me and asked, "I'm what?"

"I don't know what I'm supposed to say. I know your language, but I'm not sure how to use it to articulate what I'm feeling. All I want to do is make you happy and safe as if it's some sort of a natural, unexplainable instinct that I have. I feel like I was born with it and I have been waiting to meet you to release it."

I was startled when she got closer to me, opened her arms, and held me tightly, as she let out a wail, "Did you think we could continue living together forever?" I held her back and said, "I never planned anything for the future. I still have the heart of a dolphin, so I'm not used to humans' abilities to plan things for years to come. I know I love spending time with you, I love your laugh, your lightness, and simplicity in all matters. I know I want to protect you and I can't imagine seeing you suffer. I have experienced a sentiment with you that I can't describe, but I also don't think about its consequences or results. I don't know how to answer the 'what's next?' question. All I want right now is to return you home safely without thinking about the future."

She kept holding me, calm and unmoving, for short minutes that went by in what felt like years. Unlike what humans often claim, time passes slowly when it feels good, not when it feels dreadful. Those minutes passed slowly, for example, because I could feel thousands of heartbeats and whispers shared between us. I listened to unspoken confessions and expressed my feelings without uttering a sound. Through our rapid breaths and synchronized heartbeats, I could articulate everything I had been suppressing.

"Should I call you Ziad or Mawry?" she asked me. I said, "Is it that even a question? Ziad will always be my name since you picked it out for me." She wiped a tear off her face and said, "Are you telling me you're keeping your name just because I chose it?" "Yes." She laughed and said, "That's crazy!" to which I responded, "Is it crazier than my ability to transform into a human?" She sat down in front of her new hut and said, "Ziad, I feel confused. I'm still all over the place. Could you return to the beach and let me sleep here alone tonight?" "Of course, I just wanted to fix things to prove to you I never had any bad intentions, even though I lied to you." She said, "Alright. Just go back to the beach and let's meet first thing in the morning so we can work on the raft and leave this island." I listened to what she'd asked me and left her to sleep, but I didn't return to the beach. I simply stretched my body out in a spot that was at a short distance from her new hut, without letting her notice it.

That was the only time, as a human, that I wanted to sleep as dolphins do. I wished I could sleep with only half of my brain; however, I ended up falling into a deep sleep that came with an abundance of odd dreams that involved Arwa. I dreamt of her in strange places, wearing strange clothes and uttering incomprehensible words. I dreamt she was flying in an airship that disappeared behind thick clouds. I dreamt of her in a large house that overlooked a mountain, where she and I were exchanging words and moments of love. We were sharing soft whispers and intimate breaths as our bodies intermingled in a new dance that I had never tried before. It was a dance where we melted in each other's bodies, one that kept escalating until it reached a peak that woke me up as soon as the sun began to rise.

I got up and walked to her hut to check up on her, but I didn't find her. I quickly headed to the spring and walked alongside it while searching for her, until I finally saw her in an unexpected state: her entire body, except her face, was buried underneath the sand. Her eyes were shut and she seemed fast asleep, yet her face was reacting and responding to something only she was visualizing, while her chest went up and down as if she was physically struggling. I tried to wake her up, but she didn't respond. I tried harder, but it still didn't work out. When I gave up on trying to wake her up, I began to remove the sand off of her, but I stopped when I heard the old lady's voice, "Stop! If you remove the sand, you're going to hurt her." I turned to her questioningly, so she continued to speak, "Her body's still here, but her spirit is somewhere far away. If you want to get her back, you need to bury yourself and travel with your spirit to her." I didn't try to think or discuss anything with her, I had learned by that point that the island doesn't negotiate. I started digging the ground next to Arwa's body and quickly buried myself underneath the sand. I shut my eyes, thinking about how much I'd hurt her since the moment I met her, and how our encounter had caused more harm than good.

ARWA—MOTO MUAYA, MAY 2019

I'm not sure what had overtaken me or how I gave in to that moment of vulnerability with Ziad. How could I throw myself at him and weep on his shoulders the way I did? The way I felt towards Ziad was unmatched; I had never felt like that about anyone before. He carried an abundance of genuine feelings that most humans didn't have. I experienced "societal love" with my first husband, then I tried a zealous interest with two men after him. A zealous interest is a state that a woman enters when she is somewhat excited to get into a new experience that might snatch her from the general monotony of her life. It is a state that offers an exciting possibility, one that could develop into a relationship or even marriage. That case usually falls apart in the end, especially when it is based on rushing.

I also tried "cinematic love" with Kamel; it was flashy and showy on the outside, but hollow on the inside. The love I experienced with Ziad, however, is what I could call spiritual love. It is a love that doesn't concern itself with the future. I could call it "authentic love," as it contains the original feeling from which all love stories stem. It is a love that isn't created or destroyed, just like the law of conservation of energy. For those reasons, I made my decision to go through the experience the old lady told me about. When I asked her how I should proceed, she told me I had to bury my entire body, except for my head, underneath the sand, then I had to shut my eyes and go through with it. I followed her instructions: After burying my body underneath the sand, I gave in completely, as I took three deep inhales and fell fast asleep.

I woke up with a clenching heart. It was seven in the morning, according to that noisy classic alarm clock that made me jump with fear every morning. My phone's alarm was a much better alternative, but I have always failed to use it, even though Ali—my oldest son—has tried many times to teach me how to use it, but I always failed to apply his instructions. Ali's colleague at work called me on the phone, "Madam Nadia, please pass by Ali as soon as possible, he can't be late for work. It's labor inspection day! I will pass by you at the hospital after I'm done with work to give you Ahmed's medicine." I double-checked with her that she bought the exported medicine that the doctor had recommended, to which she affirmed, "Yes, I did. I promise." "That's great, dear. May you never experience this pain over a loved one! God bless you," I told her.

I prepared the food quickly for my other son, Ahmed. The poor boy has abstained from food for two whole days. The doctor claimed it was a sign of depression, probably caused by his long stay at the hospital and the endless pain he had to go through during his wound dressing. I prayed for him and mentioned God's holy name on his food, in hopes that it would bless it and make Ahmed finally swallow his food instead of spitting it, as he usually did those days. It has been seven years since my sons' father passed away, and ever since then, I started to play the role of both parents. Ali finished his studies in an institute of computer science, then he started working in "Obour City," whereas Ahmed, my youngest, finished high school, then quit education altogether. He began to accept any gig that came his way to make money. He was a lively, playful, and funny young man, yet he carried great responsibilities, especially since he refused the idea of his older brother paying for his living expenses.

I walked down the old staircase of the building, leaning on its old wooden handrails, then I crossed the muddy entrance in front of it. I waved at Atef, the driver of an auto-rickshaw, who was waiting for me. I opened the door of the vehicle and sat inside. "Good morning, 'Om Ali[25].' How's Ahmed?" The young driver, who was almost Ali's age, said, while sharply turning the steering wheel to set out on our ride. We drove down the steep slope of "Kabsh's Castle[26]" until we reached the main road. We were heading to Al Mounira Hospital, where my son Ahmed was getting treated in the burns depart-

[25] In some Egyptian cultures, mothers are referred to by their firstborn's name. The word "om," which means mother in Arabic, is used and followed by the firstborn's name.

[26] An old and underprivileged slum

ment. The traffic officer, Saeed, stopped us and warned Atef, like he did every morning, against his reckless driving. Auto-rickshaws were normally banned from driving on main roads, so I spoke kindly to the officer, as I always did, "Good morning, son! We apologize, I'm late for my appointment with Ahmed, and I couldn't find a taxi anywhere," to which he replied with his usual sympathy, "I understand. I hope he gets well soon," then he proceeded to scold a microbus driver who was randomly loading his passengers in the middle of the street.

I finally arrived at the hospital. Everyone there knew me, as I've been visiting the place daily for nearly two and a half months. At the burns department, my title always changed from "Om Ali" to "Om Ahmed." Ahmed was sitting on his bed, with half his body covered in gauze. Some bloody stains were beginning to appear on it, which meant it was nearly time for a new wound dressing. His face was still splotched with the burn wounds that have healed and formed scabs. Ali stood next to him, holding a juice box and begging him to drink from it, but Ahmed, as usual, refused.

I tried to offer him the food I had made him earlier, which included his favorite recipes, but he looked away, silently rejecting it. I brought a spoonful of soup to his mouth, which had become tighter since the wound healed, meaning it needed an enlargement surgery to fix it. Again, Ahmed refused to drink his soup, but this time he shouted, "I don't want it!" before he accused me and his brother of insensitivity. "I already said no." I tried to use another tactic, so I threatened to not join him in his following wound dressing if he kept rejecting his food.

He began to yell and curse at everything, especially at that unfortunate situation that made him need my help for the bare necessities—as if he hasn't needed me all his life, ever since he was born and then breastfed by me. I yelled back at him, but it quickly turned into me begging him. He still, however, rejected his food. He later broke down in tears and threatened he was going to throw up and lose his mind if he entered the wound dressing room without me.

I have been going through the same cycle for nearly two and a half months. Seventy-five days have passed since Ali came running to me in panic and, screaming, informed me that some vicious savages threw a Molotov cocktail at Ahmed in a street fight, which set his body on fire. Seventy-five days have passed since I began to stand by his side as the doctors washed his body and removed the used gauze and old cotton off of him. I watched the color of his wounds change: from brown at first, then yellow, and finally, bright red. Sometimes, an infection would make it turn blue, which perfectly encompassed the color of my sorrow over what happened to him.

After the twentieth dressing change, I began to participate in the procedure. I would help the nurse remove the cover or hand the doctor some of the supplies, while of course, maintaining my main job, which was to calm down my screaming son. I would ask him to remain patient and strong, then I had to accept his accusations when he would call me insensitive. He would remind me I wasn't in his shoes, so it didn't make sense for me to be judging him or asking for patience. What he didn't know was that every thread of gauze they removed would tear my heart out. Ahmed never used to be disrespectful to me, but he wasn't being himself. Seventy-five days went by, but the pain remained the same. Almost half his wounds have healed, but the rest were getting excessively critical as if they were punishing the ones that healed. Every time I held and kissed his hand, promising him it was all going to be over soon and that the hardest part had passed, I would be lying to him. He and I both knew that.

A new doctor had arrived on that day! He seemed stern; his looks were sharp and he didn't speak much. He asked the team to change Ahmed's urinary catheter (for the twelfth time) and change his intravenous needle (for the fiftieth time), then attach a venous access device in his neck (after he spent a month without one, as the previous one had caused an infection that almost killed him). Then he ordered the team to put a tube inside his nose to supply him with nutrients, which made me break down. I tried to explain to him how horrendous that tube was for Ahmed the last time it was attached. I never complained during any of the seventy-five wound dressing sessions, and I never opened my mouth about those painful stitches that penetrated his skin, alongside my soul, even if I had silently counted them one by one. That feeding tube, however, was always torture, even if it was good for my son.

I tried to speak with his previous doctor, "Please, Dr. Bishoy, I beg you. I know you care for Ahmed and you look out for him as if he was your own brother. Please, talk to the new doctor and ask him not to do it," but he said, "I can't do anything about it. He's the new department chief, we have to follow his orders." And that was how we started a new cycle of agony that started with the placement of the tube. I was surprised when the new doctor later summoned me to his office, but I headed to him, secretly wishing him the worst. He was sitting on a couch, in the presence of Dr. Bishoy, and he asked me to sit down. He first proceeded to explain why he insisted on inserting the feeding tube for Ahmed and how it was beneficial for him, but I listened to him without paying much attention. I knew how much they loved to create elaborate reasons and excuses, without doing much effort. My poor boy was in pain and his life was in jeopardy, but they didn't do much about it. I was shocked, however, to hear from that new doctor, that he wanted to remove a section from my older son's skin and transplant it to his brother's body. I stared at him as if he had just lost his mind. What kind of nonsense was that? And how come no one proposed his precious suggestion before if it was that revolutionary? Did he imply he wanted to risk both of my sons' lives? "No way! My son Ali works to spend on his brother. He's the one who buys his medicine and he's the one who looks after him when I'm gone. What if complications happen? What am I supposed to do then?" I said frantically.

The stern doctor spoke sharply, "Listen, Madam Nadia." He spoke my name without the title "Om Ahmed" or "Om Ali," which, for some reason, made his words sound even more petrifying. "Your son will die if his brother doesn't donate part of his skin to him." "God forbid that should ever happen. God, how are you so cruel?" Dr. Bishoy then intervened, apologizing to his boss on my behalf and attempting to calm me down at the same time. He tried to persuade me with the idea, so I suggested that I donate the skin instead of Ali. "Not possible. You're a hepatitis C patient, that's why you couldn't donate blood earlier," he told me. I stood up, looking at the new doctor in disdain, and said, "I don't accept this risk. I heard you studied in the West, so figure out another way that doesn't involve making me lose my mind over my two sons."

Ali approached me later that same day and begged me to accept the doctor's proposal. When I persistently refused, he teared up and said, "Are we just going to let Ahmed die?" I scolded him, "That doctor is insane and he's speaking gibberish." "No, he's using the knowledge he gained in the West to help Ahmed." I patted Ali on the back and said, "We're not like them, dear. We're thick-skinned and we can handle much worse." He didn't like what I said and went back to begging me. "I'm donating to my brother whether you like it or not!" he eventually told me. I swore that if he did that, I was going to starve myself until I stopped breathing.

One son was enough for me to worry about. It was already more than I could handle. Not only was I concerned about the potential failure of the surgery, but I was also terrified of witnessing my two sons whimper in pain at the same time. No, my heart wouldn't be able to handle a scream from Ahmed then a sob from Ali, as I did nothing but sit between the two of them in utter helplessness. Ali kept begging and begging, before another doctor interfered and tried to persuade me on her part. I asked her if it was guaranteed that Ahmed was going to die without the transplant or if it was guaranteed that he would survive if his brother donated to him, to which she said, "It's all in God's hands, Om Ahmed. We only try our best." so I snapped, "Then I'm sure God wouldn't want me to risk both of my sons' lives for something that may or may not happen." Then I looked at Ali, "Listen, you're not even allowed to speak about this anymore. And don't you dare tell your brother about it."

After that, things began to calm down and everyone ended up submitting to my wishes. During the following couple of days, things mostly remained the same, except that Ahmed finally managed to gain a couple of kilos after he was fed through the tube. One day, however, he suddenly began to hallucinate. He was recounting random events from his childhood and speaking to his deceased father as if he could see him right in front of him. In no time, he was put on a ventilator by his doctors, who began to forbid me from being with him, except during his wound dressing. He was dying, so he couldn't feel the pain of the wound dressing anymore, or that's what I thought. Eventually, the machines in the hospitals beeped, painfully announcing his death. The doctors rushed into the room and tried to resuscitate him, but to no avail.

I initially confronted the news of his death somewhat steadily, until Ali arrived in the hospital and saw his only brother lying dead. He broke down, immediately accusing me of killing his brother. I initially didn't understand what he meant, until he screamed, "You should have let me donate my skin to him. You're the reason he's dead." I froze in my place in shock after hearing his words. The whole world fell apart right in front of me. I fell to the ground, trying to comprehend the situation while covering my face between my hands. I heard the stern doctor's voice calming Ali down, "Your brother's condition was critical. He could have still passed away even if you donated your skin. His hour has come, so you can't carry the guilt of his death on your shoulders or accuse your mother." It was too late, Ali's accusations had already come out of his mouth like a pistol that was shot straight to my heart, shattering it and draining my soul in the process. I felt the air escape my chest, and I couldn't let it back in again. Everything turned dark, while I shivered in helplessness.

I opened my eyes. I'm still Arwa! I'm not Om Ahmed or Om Ali, but I could still feel the pain of a stab inside my chest. It wasn't a dream, it was truly my life and my decision to kill that young man. Even if the doctor tried to claim otherwise, it was still my fault. How excruciating was it to lose one son and be loathed by the other! I killed a person. Yes, losing a son was agonizing, but carrying the guilt of killing him made it much harder. I couldn't believe I did that! I, Arwa, chose to let Ahmed die before I forced everyone to help me do it. That's all I could feel. It felt as if I was truly that Nadia lady, even though I knew I was Arwa. How cruel was that damned island to me, and that old lady as well! Or was I supposed to solely blame myself and my terrible decision-making? I didn't deserve to be a mother and I wouldn't be able to lose a son or handle the potential guilt of making any wrong decision afterward.

The world was spinning. I tried to move my arm so I could get out of that voluntary grave, but I couldn't do it. Maybe I didn't have the energy to. At that point, I didn't want anything from life anymore. I closed my eyes in surrender, then pictured myself sitting in a small room of an old house. I heard an explosion outside, which made the house shake. I crouched down in fear and shouted, "Where am I?" I heard the old lady's voice respond, saying, "You're in a small town that is occupied and going through a fierce war. Ziad is coming to save you, but he might die on his way to do it. If he does, his blood will remain on your hand, just like you killed poor Ahmed with your stubbornness and defective convictions. If Ziad dies trying to save you, he will die in real life too, and you will live with the guilt of not one, but two evildoings. Moreover, you'll have to bury Ziad's body yourself."

ZIAD—UNNAMED CITY, UNSPECIFIED TIME

I was inside my house, which was built on the outskirts of a city I didn't know. Arwa was also staying in the same city, but at another house in one of the central towns that were constantly getting bombed. The sound of explosions made my heart pound out of my chest. I was sure it was a battle between two equally fanatical parties that were determined to take over a piece of land, even if they had turned it into piles of rubble and corpses. I had to remind myself it was nothing but a mere illusion created by the island.

I have already learned so much about the different wars that humans have gotten themselves into, where they killed thousands, sometimes millions, of innocent souls for the pettiest and most absurd reasons. In fact, the reasons behind all wars drastically contradict what humans usually pride themselves on. Learning about wars, however, is one thing, and living one, is a different story. Everything I have learned about the history of humans never triggered the same nauseous feeling that spread all over my body when I first heard the sounds of bombs and bullets, especially as I knew how each one getting fired tore apart at least one human body with its eruption. I heard the firing of a cannon, followed by multiple shorter-sounding shootings. I wondered: Which one killed more souls? The one that made the extremely loud sound or the consecutive shorter shots? Which one posed a greater danger to Arwa's life? Did any of those bombs hurt her, or at least the version of her that existed in that city?

The island told me I had to rescue her. I had to go to the house where her soul was trapped, and once we physically touched one another, everything would finally come to an end. She would get rid of the sorrow and guilt that she felt, and she would be liberated from the terror she had experienced due to the bombs, as well as her concern over my safety. The old lady informed me, "If you're able to reach her safely, you will cure her of everything she agreed to go through for your sake. She will only remember you and the love you have for one another, without the pain and guilt linked with the experience. As for you, you will live to be among the rare ones, the superior species that can transform into a dolphin or a human whenever and wherever they desire." I asked her, "What if I fail?" "There's no such thing as failure, you'll rescue her from the agony just by participating in the experience. If you die on your way to save her, you will lose your privilege and go back to being a regular dolphin. You will forget about her and the same goes for her. She will return to Bora Bora and remember nothing except that she fell in the ocean but was luckily saved."

I didn't have a choice but to participate in the experience, since that alone was going to save her from the pain she went through for my sake. Even if I failed to save her, it was enough for me to return her home safely and erase the hardships she went through from her head. The distance between where I was and her house was a long one, and the bombing wasn't subsiding. I could innately visualize the map of the city inside my head as if I was truly born there. I went out to the streets and began to walk near the walls, trying to protect myself as much as I could. There were no pedestrians, which meant they were all in hiding, and most of the buildings were destroyed by the bombs and shootings. I could only see what was left of them through the holes in the walls. I contemplated the noiseless destruction that was only interrupted by the sound of bombs. What did they get out of this? And where was everyone? Did everyone get buried underneath the rubble or did they escape the city, fearing for their lives?

I didn't understand how the "fighting" actually worked. Did the two parties stand on opposite sides and then begin shooting at each other, and after they were finished, they would start counting bodies? Maybe whoever killed a bigger number of bodies would be announced winner? When a fight occurs in the world of dolphins, the side that is bigger in number will usually win and that's it. Humans, however, have more complicated rules. I thought about the different possibilities before my thoughts were interrupted by the sound of a vehicle that let out a loud siren, emitting striking colors that were quite visible despite the daylight. I began to understand it was an ambulance car, so I immediately prayed it wasn't going to rescue Arwa from some sort of danger. The thought alone made me walk faster.

I was approaching an area where the sound of shootings resonated loudly, so I told myself I had to think strategically about what to do. I suddenly remembered there was a longer route, distant from the shootings, that could get me to Arwa's house, so I swerved to the first alley that took me to the new route. I felt more reassured when the noises were beginning to fade away, so I began to walk slower to catch my breath, but I didn't stop walking altogether, of course. Suddenly, I tripped and fell on my face. When I placed my hands on the ground to try and get back up, my hand accidentally came across a human body.

It was a corpse! His body was still warm, surrounded by a pool of blood that started from the side of his head, where he was shot. It was my first time seeing a murdered human. There was no time for me to contemplate what I had seen or even take in the shock. I was on an urgent mission, so I had to get a grip and pull myself together. Suddenly, I heard an overwhelming roaring sound, then felt a bullet whizz by my side. I didn't know how to react, so I hurriedly got up and headed to a winding street. It reminded me of when I used to escape tiger sharks in the ocean. The sound of shootings was still buzzing around me until I finally saw a barrier, made of barrels, that was surrounded by armed men. They aimed their rifles at me before one of them said to me, "Stop."

I froze. One of them asked, "Who are you? You don't look familiar." "Please sir, I am trying to rescue a sick woman who is stuck in the center of the city." The man looked at me skeptically and asked, "Where are you from?" to which I answered, "I'm a journalist from Peru. I left my colleague here two days ago, and I need to get her back." The man laughed sarcastically and said, "You want to risk your life for a colleague?" then he smiled as viciously as an orca that was about to attack a baby humpback whale. He swung a punch at me that brought me down to the ground.

I was so enraged that I almost attacked him back, despite all the weapons that he and his team possessed, before I remembered how much I was going to lose if I died inside that city. I was going to go back to being a dolphin that feeds on fish and plays around with his pod, forgetting everything I have learned and experienced. The thought itself terrified me. One of the armed men dragged me on the ground to the nearest wall. He then sat me up, kicked me, and asked, "Who are you? Speak!" When I repeated my story, he kicked me again, then grabbed me by my neck, propped me up, and stuck my face against the wall. He sniffed at me like I was prey he was about to attack. "Are you trying to tell me you're not one of those fools who come here from the other side of the world to join our enemies' line?" he asked me. I pretended to be crying in fear and said, "I never even touched a weapon my whole life. Please let me go." He held me by my head and beat it against the wall multiple times while cursing me with words I didn't even understand. He then let me fall to the ground, dizzy and helpless.

I heard another voice ask that insane bastard about my identity, so he answered him. "I don't believe what he's saying." "He does look like he's from Latin America, he has their features." The aggressive man then said, "I think we should keep him until we're sure." They kept me lying on the ground for around half an hour, as they proceeded to move around and talk without glancing twice at me. I thought about escaping, because the longer I stayed the longer Arwa suffered, and the possibility of me ending up dead further increased as well. I tried to sit up, but I was given a surprise kick that brought me back to the ground.

As much as I was physically in pain, I was much more invested in my contempt and disdain for those creatures. I thought about how some humans actually lived similar experiences in real life, not just in an island's creation. How can a human handle being degraded that way, as if he was a piece of garbage or a dangerous moss that had to be extracted? In fact, how could anyone, like that aggressive man, for instance, live with all that hatred and lewdness inside him? What instinct pushed humans to behave that way? The most honorable feature I would have if I fully became a human, is that I would be free of that horrendous instinct. I wasn't born human and I wasn't breastfed with human milk; I was sure it had to be something they were fed that shaped them to become that way.

I spent a long time trying to gather all my focus and energy so I could find a way to escape. I saw the other man, who thought I was Latin American, standing nearby. I whispered to him in a drained voice, begging him to listen to me. He asked bleakly, "What do you want?" "I swear I have nothing to do with—" My sentence was cut short by a loud shooting sound, then I was drowned by heavy ash covered in blood. The man's body suddenly fell over me, followed by a crazy orchestra of rifles that went off everywhere.

ARWA—UNNAMED CITY, UNSPECIFIED TIME

I sank to the ground, burying my face between my hands. The texture of the rug beneath me felt rough against the soles of my feet. The explosions that were going off, only hundreds of meters away, violently shook the walls of the house. The old lady's words took over my thoughts, especially when she claimed I was responsible for Ziad's life. Suddenly, those thoughts were replaced by an image of Ahmed's painful demise, followed by Ali furiously shouting at me. I didn't understand how any of it was happening! Did my soul inhabit Om Ahmed's in a way that allowed me to make that decision instead of her? Was I having an exceedingly realistic dream?

Whatever the real answer was, I knew I could recall painful events that happened in her life even before the dream itself took place, as if they were memories from my own life. I could remember the death of her husband and the long years of loneliness, deprivation, and poverty that followed after his death. I remembered how she moved out of her nice, comfortable house to a suffocating, narrow burrow. I could even remember the day she heard the news about Ahmed's fight, accompanied by the agonizing days that followed it. Every time a memory related to his pain or suffering popped in my head, I also recalled the day she gave birth to him. It was such a long and tiresome delivery, that the gynecologist eventually had to use vacuum extraction to help guide him out of her body.

I couldn't fight the grief I felt for Ahmed, but I was able to resist the old lady's attempt to make me feel guilty towards Ziad. I didn't force him to participate in the experiment. Moreover, I had agreed to go through all that heartache for him, regardless of my true motive: whether I loved him or I only wanted to return the favor of him saving my life. As I was pondering over the situation, an extremely close explosion nearly ruptured my eardrum, shattering the window's glasses into thousands of pieces. Flying pieces of shrapnel touched my body, so I shook them off in a panic, wondering if any of the horrendous explosions I heard happened to hurt Ziad. Another nearby explosion shook the entire building. Through the window, I could see the entire side of a building completely collapse, accompanied by screams and shouted warnings.

The old woman didn't mention anything about what would happen if I died. Was I going to die in reality as well, or was I going to survive but lose Ziad, putting an end to the experience altogether? Was it nothing more than a lesson to teach me that my old problems were too trivial to even mention? When I recalled the hardest moments of my real life and compared them to Nadia's, I realized that what people claimed about happiness and sadness being equally divided upon all human beings in different ways, was complete nonsense. Nadia's share of sadness was certainly larger than mine. Then I compared the cruelest moments of Nadia's life to one moment of terror that the women screaming downstairs were experiencing, and realized they were living a struggle much worse than hers. I clung to that last thought as it made me listen harder to a woman screaming for help downstairs. I crawled towards the window, trying to avoid the glassy shrapnel, and carefully took a look.

I saw her and realized that part of her body was buried underneath the rubble. She was desperately trying to separate the fragments to get out, as she screamed for help. She suddenly looked up at me, which startled me and made me fall on my back, where shrapnel penetrated my shoulder. I removed it, screaming in pain. I looked around for something that could work as a bandage, but the woman downstairs wouldn't stop screaming, "Please help my little girl. Everyone escaped, there's no one but you." Her little daughter! I didn't see or hear any kids in the area, which meant the woman was certainly lying. "Please, she'll die. I don't want—" before she could continue her sentence, another explosion went off. Everything became quiet. I looked out of the window again and saw the woman looking around frantically as if she was trying to make sure the explosion didn't take away her life. She then looked up at me again and begged, "Please…" she looked down at the fragments of rubble beneath her and spoke in a clear voice, that she tried to make as reassuring as possible, "Don't be scared, sweetie. Mom will get you out."

I couldn't take it anymore! I opened the door of the house and hurried down the stairs. I didn't run into anyone, as if they had all suddenly vanished. I went out through the building's door and walked to the other side. Most buildings around me were either entirely destroyed or only had one side standing. I finally reached the woman and began to help her get out, but she stopped me and asked me to help her daughter instead. "She went quiet, I don't know what's going on," she wept. She pointed to another spot, a tiny opening among the rubble. I looked inside it and found a little girl, barely five years old, completely covered in ashes and dust. I swept the dust off of her face and realized she was breathing regularly, but she wasn't moving. Her cheeks had some abrasions on them, but they couldn't conceal the innocence of her angelic face. Her feet were stuck underneath the heavy piles of rubble, so when I tried to get her out, she winced in pain. I was mad at myself for hurting her, so I hurriedly began to remove the dust, soil, ashes, and rocks, and eventually a large piece of concrete, underneath of which her feet were stuck.

I began to drag her out gently while supporting her broken leg until I finally got her out of the gap completely. The child, however, had passed out again. Her mother was still crying, as she desperately tried to get a word or a response out of her, but the child remained silent. I tried to help the woman as well, but she spoke to me in a weak voice, "Please leave me and just take my kid to the nearest hospital." I tried to convince her to let me help her, but she refused and said, "There's no time. The doctors need to see her, now."

I froze, not knowing what to do. If I took the child to the hospital, Ziad could arrive at the house and not find me inside. There was no possible justification, however, for abandoning that poor kid and letting her die. I thought about how everything in this scenario was fictional, which meant there was never a dying kid in the first place. I asked myself, "Yet what if this is really happening? What if I truly came here by magical means and happened to be in a real setting? That means the child is certainly going to die." Even if it was a minor possibility, leaving a child on the brink of death wasn't an option.

I carried her. I asked the woman for directions to the hospital, so she pointed with her arm to the main road, which had a demolished building by its street corner. She mentioned that the hospital was at the end of that road, around a kilometer away. I began to walk hurriedly while maintaining a proper distance between me and the buildings to my sides, afraid that one might collapse at any time. I entered the main road, which, to my surprise, had more undestroyed buildings than the other streets. I began to walk faster to get to the hospital, even though the young girl winced in pain every time her broken leg bumped against mine. Even though she was in pain, it was still a good sign.

I heard the echo of an explosion. I looked behind me and realized it hit a building I had just passed by, so I thanked God and walked faster. I heard the sound of a projectile getting fired, followed by another explosion that went off nearby, flinging me down to the ground as

I held on tightly to the girl. She didn't scream that time, which terrified me. I tried to wake her up as I remained crouched near the explosion spot. A plane with an irritating noise soared above us, followed by some smaller, repetitive blasts that woke the girl up and made me scurry towards the hospital.

I was terrified. I realized Ziad could potentially be one of the victims of those explosions. I didn't, however, have any time to ponder the different possibilities, as I was soon startled by a loud bang of an explosion to the north. Another one blazed behind me, followed by a second, then a third. More explosions took place, making me scurry as if they carried the same effect of a whip used by a wagoner against an abused horse's back. I fell to the ground, which made the poor young girl shriek in pain. I let out useless apologies as I carried on along the way until I finally reached the hospital, where I saw the ultimate surprise.

ZIAD—UNDETERMINED TIME AND PLACE

I had instinctively realized, or maybe through a piece of information I was taught by the island, that if you ever found yourself caught in the middle of a shooting, you had to closely attach yourself to the ground, then crawl away from the clash until you could find a shelter or at least a wall to protect yourself behind. I carefully started to crawl, as the cracking sound of the bullets traveled from my ear to the convulsions of my brain. I saw one of the armed men—the aggressive one who had humiliated me earlier—carrying his weapon and firing frantically, as his eyes searched for a shelter to hide behind. His face looked terrified as if he was expecting a bullet to penetrate his body at any given moment.

A bullet scratched the skin of my back while another grazed the top of my head, both causing horrendous pain and minor bleeding. I was able, however, to finally hide behind a brick wall. The aggressive armed man was still switching between shooting and retreating.

His eyes were widened and his jaw intensely clenched, such that it almost looked like his teeth were about to break at any minute. His arms quivered with every bullet that his weapon was firing. After some time, he fell to the ground, covered in his blood, then he started to crawl in my direction.

It was my first time to witness someone dying. He breathed rapidly, coughing blood out of his mouth like scattered spray mixed with his saliva. I didn't know what to do. The man was groaning in pain, sobbing, begging, and speaking to me, using words I couldn't understand. I tried to comprehend what he was saying, but the words were disrupted by the gargling of blood in his throat. I felt sorry for him. Only short minutes ago, he stomped on the ground as if he owned it. He kicked and beat me in dominance and assertion. Suddenly, he turned into a desperate child, but instead of crying for candy, he was begging for more air so he could breathe.

Wars, as written in novels and history books, are nothing compared to one moment of what I had witnessed. How could writers and historians summarize wars by dates and numbers? There is so much more to them. That one man, for instance, could be perceived by some as a heartless criminal and by others as a hero. What my eyes saw, however, was a helpless child in tears, dying on his mother's lap. He was no different from a baby humpback whale that was viciously getting attacked by orcas, as he pleadingly looked at his helpless mother.

He died. He took his last breath, as the blood that ran from his body took any sign of life away with it. He became completely still, as if he turned from a vigorous and strong living creature to worm food in a matter of seconds. When the shooting somewhat settled down, I began to crawl away from the battlefield. Finally, it came to an end. Perhaps the two parties gave up on taking control over that particular piece of land and decided to call it a day after murdering a number of its inhabitants.

I continued going my way. I glimpsed a figure of a man who could hardly walk, as a string of blood followed his footsteps. The moment I walked past him, he fell to the ground and called out for me in a hoarse voice, "Save me, son." I turned around and saw his old, wrinkled face. It seemed like he was among the unfortunate people that happened to be present on the battlefield, and one of the bullets decided to graze him. "Please take me to the hospital," he asked me. I sat down beside him and began to examine him. The back of his thigh was heavily bleeding, but I didn't know what to do. He suddenly took off the leather belt he was wearing and asked me to tie it around his leg so it could stop the bleeding, which I did. He screamed in pain, then he spoke, panting in fear, "Thank you, son. You helped stop the bleeding. Now, please help me get up and walk me to the hospital." I said, "I'm on an urgent mission, I can't be late." "Is it so urgent that you're going to leave an old man in the street to die?" he asked me.

I wasn't sure what to do. Do I leave that poor old man to face his destiny alone? Or do I make Arwa wait even longer and risk the possibility of her house getting bombed? The island old lady didn't clarify what was going to happen to Arwa in the event that she died, and I forgot to ask in the middle of everything else going on.

All I knew was that letting her die in that place could be extremely risky. Accompanying the man to the hospital was going to increase the possibility of that risk. Projectiles were propelled from more than one direction, which meant that any random one could easily destroy the house that Arwa awaited me in.

"Don't let me die, son. You look like a good person," the old man said.

I was going to be at least an hour late if I took him to the hospital. I was consumed by my desire and longing to meet Arwa as much as I wanted to make sure she was safe. Both those instincts were compelling me to leave the man and continue on my way. "You weren't even supposed to be here, it's like you were never here in the first place," a voice in my head would say, then it would get fought by another voice that said, "But it's not right to assume that. Who knows? Maybe you were meant to be here so you could save his life. Perhaps saving Arwa is just an additional task." I felt like I was hallucinating or losing control of myself. I took a moment to breathe and absorb things wisely. "Let go of everything and return to your roots. Go back to being a dolphin and judge the situation out of context." As soon as I followed that train of thought, it all became clear to me. It wasn't even an option to let the old man die, especially given that Arwa was waiting in a closed shelter.

I held the old man up and asked him to lean on me, then we began walking slowly towards the hospital. He told me, "You're a good gentleman. You remind me of my son! Oh, how I miss him. And his wife and kids too. My grandkids are the apples of my eyes." "Where did your son go?" I asked, scared that his answer might be something along the lines of: "They're all buried underneath the rubble." Thankfully, however, he said, "They migrated like everyone else." "Then why did you stay?" "This land is a piece of me. I can't leave it," he said as an outburst of blasts went off. "What about your son and grandkids? Aren't they also—" My question was interrupted by the sound of a loud explosion. The old man smiled at me, encouraging me to continue asking my question. "Isn't your family a piece of you as well?" "They are. But this country is an unmoving land that my body is attached to, so I can't separate myself from it. As for my son and grandkids, they are free, moving creatures." "But the land's destroyed. It's no longer the same as before," I told him. He said, "Even if it turns into a dump or a ruin, it'll always be my land." "Is that why they're killing each other? For the land?" I asked. He said, "Lands don't offer anyone life or death. They kill each other for their own greedy purposes."

We silently approached the hospital, as his words made me speechless. Whenever I tried to understand humans, I felt more conflicted by them. No wonder even they didn't understand one another. Each person has a different world built inside his head, completely dissimilar to his brother's world. I didn't know whether the old man's words made sense or not, and I probably never will. The stored wisdom that the land provided me with was one thing, but the gained wisdom I acquired through my experience with humans was another. It became clear to me that books didn't only fail in describing wars, they also failed to describe a sentiment as simple as the one that man was expressing to me. Furthermore, no book could convey the way my heart was impacted by his words and genuine voice, especially when he talked about his land or when he justified his family's absence.

We finally entered the hospital, which turned out to be complete chaos. People were running in hundreds of directions, as wounded and injured patients were lying on the floor. I helped the man rest his body on a small bed. A young wounded man was sitting on it earlier, but he got up as soon as he saw the old man and offered it to him, out of respect for his age. I left him and began looking for a doctor. After I found one and he began to examine the old man, I turned the other way and intended to leave the hospital, without even saying goodbye. I had done what I came here to do. The man, however, called out for me, held my hand, patted it, then thanked me. I wasn't sure what to tell him before I suddenly heard Arwa's voice, "Ziad! Oh my God, Ziad."

I turned around and there she was. Her face and clothes were ashy and she was carrying a little girl on her shoulder. I ran towards her and was about to hug her, but the child's body came between us. I took her from Arwa and ran back towards the doctors room, where someone guided me on where to find the children's ward. I put her on one of the examination tables there, where a doctor and a nurse arrived and began to examine her and deal with her injuries. As soon as I got out of the room, I found Arwa waiting for me outside, with a yearning smile and teary eyes.

ARWA—UNNAMED CITY, UNSPECIFIED TIME

My eyes fell on Ziad, who was standing in the corridor of the hospital, speaking to a doctor and checking on an old man who sat on a shabby seat. I could see humanity thriving in him. He had evolved in my eyes from only being a fantastical creature on a magical island to a real human being. I realized we were more similar than I had thought, as he was also carrying out a humane act with that old man, just like I chose to bring the little girl to the hospital, despite knowing it could diminish my chances of being rescued by Ziad.

I called out his name. At that point, I was bewildered and exhausted, and I needed a doctor or a nurse to help me with the girl. I couldn't, however, help but call Ziad's name. He turned around and his face immediately lit up. He ran towards me, past the bodies of people who chaotically moved in all directions. He was about to hold me but stopped himself when he glimpsed the child hanging on my shoulder. He carefully took her from me, then ran off to search for someone who could examine her as I followed him. He was dealing with the situation instinctively and effortlessly as if he was a regular volunteer at the hospital. My heart shivered in awe as we stood together to help save other people's lives. I watched him as he carefully and gently put the child down on the bed, then proceeded to speak to the doctor and learn about her condition. It was like watching a dream unfold right in front of me: was he born a dolphin, or has he always been that perfectly wholesome human?

After making sure the little girl was okay, Ziad ran towards me. He had infinite nobility, genuineness, and honesty inside him, and loads of ashes and dust all over his clothes. He pulled me close to his chest, where I felt his longing, tenderness, and kindness. It was a genuine hug that took place in the middle of chaos, crowds, and explosions. I felt so safe between his arms that I began to forget about the pain from before. I let go of the sorrow that was caused by "Om Ahmed's" experience, as I felt it turn into an ancient memory that the passage of years erased. Even the horror I experienced in the unnamed city had transformed into reassurance, converting any doubt I had about my feelings towards him into ultimate certainty.

I stepped back and said, "There's something we must do before we get back." "What is it?" "The little girl's mother is still stuck under the rubble. We have to get her out and bring her here," I told him. He stood hesitantly then asked, "Is this place even real, Arwa?" to which I instantly replied, "I don't know, but we can't risk it, just like you couldn't risk that old man's life." He grabbed me by the hand and asked me where she was, then we left the hospital together. I felt some viscosity between his hand and mine, and when we looked at the source, we saw blood oozing from my wound. "Let's go back and cover it with a bandage," he suggested, but I refused and insisted on keeping moving instead.

The mother was still in the same state that I had left her in. Her head tilted back as if she had given up. The street was empty and the bombings had stopped, so the sound of our footsteps alarmed her. She opened her eyes and asked about her daughter, in a quavering voice I could barely hear. When we assured her that she was fine, she sighed in relief, "Thank God!" We began to help her, while she continued to thank us and express her gratitude. We worked on removing the rubble until it was nearly nighttime. During that time, everything was quiet and no one showed up, as if everyone had forgotten about the city altogether. Ziad removed pieces of concrete off of her with sweat covering his entire face and arms. I contemplated him in admiration, as I held the woman to my chest and proceeded to console her for the excruciating pain she was in. Whenever Ziad would notice my lovestruck looks at him, he would give me a short, yet meaningful smile. I felt like I was gifted a rare, beautiful, tender flower.

We finally managed to get her out. Ziad dragged her outside of the pile as she held on to me until we managed to leave the area of the building. He then carried her and we began to walk back to the hospital. We saw an abandoned car with one door open, so I entered it and tried to start the car in hopes of making the journey easier for us. I asked Ziad to gently let the woman down on the ground until I could figure out how to start it. It was a Lada, similar to an old one I had when I was younger, so I could manage to start it. We carried the woman and stretched her body out on the backseat, then began to move slowly on the main road to the hospital. Some people were starting to show up, but before I could question the reason, I saw them form lines to try and buy food resources.

When we finally arrived at the hospital, Ziad asked me to wait for him outside, as he claimed we had to make sure the car didn't go anywhere, so it would be easier for us to return. I refused his idea and, instead, simply took the keys and shut the door, as if the car had belonged to us all along. A few steps before the entrance, we heard the buzzing of a missile, which in no time shook the ground and pushed the three of us towards the hospital's gate. The car caught on fire, which made me explode with rage. I began to curse and scream for no reason.

We entered the hospital alongside others that were seeking refuge. Ziad put the woman down on one of the beds and proceeded to look for her daughter so he could further reassure her as if he was determined to finish the task till its very end. I would feel terrified the minute he walked away from me as if he was going to vanish forever. I felt like a mother who was saying goodbye to her child on his first day of school. Ziad was gone for such a long time that I began to count seconds the way I was taught by my swimming coach as a kid: "One thousand and one, one thousand and two, one thousand forty-five, one thousand and seventy." When I reached the number "one thousand two hundred and eight," he finally showed up. I felt upset and wanted to ask what took him that long, even though it didn't make sense for me to ask such a question, but during the time he was away from me, I could feel myself running out of breath.

We weren't allowed to exit the hospital. The rate of bombing had reached its peak and the shootings wouldn't stop. We talked to the gatekeeper and explained to him that we needed to get back to the house, but he said, "You and your husband did a wonderful job. Even though you're both strangers here, you still helped a poor mother and her daughter, and he saved one of my uncles. The least we could do is provide you with a shelter to stay at tonight." I would normally blush at the fact that he called us a married couple, but I was too tired and my feet could barely keep me standing. The man didn't wait for us to respond, he simply pointed to one of the workers and told him to lead us.

We followed the man as he climbed down some short stairs that led to a basement. We then walked in a narrow corridor and he opened a door for us. It was an old, neglected room, with a bunch of random items scattered on its floor. The room had two coverless beds and a small bathroom. As soon as the man closed the door, I was overwhelmed by an urge to forget everything and immediately hug Ziad, which he seemed to be thinking about as well. I forgot about my tired legs and the exhaustion that took over my entire body, and simply let my soul dissolve in his arms. I stepped back, sat on the bed, and let myself melt with Ziad in a moment of pure adoration that extended to every cell of our bodies. I knew that my real body was buried underneath the sand in Moto Muaya, that's why I didn't concern myself with the extent of what could happen between us or what was considered acceptable and what wasn't.

It was the best reward I had received from that soul-traveling journey. I finally acted upon all those moments of suppression, longing, and craving that I experienced with him. It wasn't a typical dream, since it was a shared moment between both of us—between me and him or, more accurately, me and myself. We were one, inhabiting two different bodies. I never experienced the magic of physical love the way I experienced it with Ziad. With him, I learned, even though I had been married twice, that physical love is an extension of a spiritual connection; it extends from it and supports it at the same time. I couldn't compare what I had with him to what I had with Kamel, for instance. With Kamel, our connection was a seemingly perfect picture taken with a smartphone but with Ziad, it felt like an original painting drawn by da Vinci. The difference was as drastic as the difference between a random selfie that Lisa del Giocondo took of herself and the *Mona Lisa* painting that Leonardo da Vinci painted of her. With Ziad, our moments were shared and owned by both of us, but with Kamel, our moments were nothing but additional photos taken by his personal lens. The beauty of Ziad's painting resided in every brushstroke, every color, and every shiver of an art-loving hand.

I spent the entire night with him. The room's window was close to the ceiling, and it overlooked the surface of the road. It was made of cloudy glass that sometimes transferred the blinks of explosions, the lights of missiles, and the sound of shootings. Ziad and I, however, were separate from everything else taking place. He was exploring his human half with me, while I was exploring my whole self with him.

36

MOTO MUAYA—MAY 2019

ZIAD

I woke up on the island. It turned out we didn't have to head back to the house where Arwa initially stayed because the minute morning arrived in that unnamed city, my vision became blurry, everything went dark, our long embrace softened, and we found ourselves buried underneath the island's sand. I got up quickly and helped Arwa get up as well while dusting the sand off of her, but she pushed me away bashfully and continued doing it herself.

I, myself, felt shy as well. What happened between the two of us felt too real to be part of a dream. I didn't know the city's name and I didn't recognize the accent or even features of its people, but I knew they were certainly Arabs. The experience, whether it was imaginary or not, left me with many opposing thoughts about humans. They worship life and destroy it to the core at the same time. They are both kind and heartless. Cruel and delicate. They are the definition of everything and its opposite. I couldn't be sure if anything that happened was real, but the hours I spent in Arwa's arms definitely felt like it. Every touch of hers irrevocably affected my soul. If anything, humans are the luckiest, because they get to experience those feelings and sensations better than any other creature in the world.

We headed to the water source, where we washed our faces while exchanging shy glances. She suddenly said, "It was a dream!" I nodded, so she said, "We're … I … I'm hungry." She looked at the water, filled the palms of her hands with it, then drank from it. "Welcome back, our war heroes," a new voice spoke to us. I turned around, to find out that the voice belonged to a young woman, who somewhat resembled the old lady. She looked like she could be her daughter. Arwa asked, "Who are you?" "I'm the spirit of the island," the lady answered her. She then took a glance at herself and said, laughing, "Only, I'm a little younger now." I said in shock, "A lot younger! Where are your two sisters?" "In the cave, as they always are. We want you to go there now."

I walked behind her, unsure of what was going on. What could she possibly want? Was the island done testing us, or were there more experiments in store? When I arrived at the cave and then entered it, I noticed how it appeared untypically enchanting. There was a comfortable, colorful couch instead of the usual branch. The woman sat between her two sisters, who had also become young ladies, and began to talk, "You followed all the steps, Ziad. You fell in love with a woman and she loved you back. She's someone who accepted to go through difficult and sad experiences for your sake. And in return, you agreed to participate in a dangerous experience, where both of you proved your good nature and pure intentions."

I appreciated her feedback, but I was too focused on another question that I had in my head. "Will her love make her want to stay with me forever?" I asked. The woman said, "Your love for one another revealed hidden aspects that were buried deep down. It's the kind of love that changes one's perception of life. You always loved her without questioning the fate of that love, so what changed and made you think about tomorrow?" I didn't know the answer, so I didn't speak. She said, "Perhaps experiencing life with Arwa outside of the island changed your perspective, especially when—" She let out a playful laugh without continuing her sentence, which made me understand she was referring to the night that we slept over at the hospital.

"Anyway, here's what you must know." She continued speaking, with a solemn look on her face. "You have officially become a human dolphin. That means you can change your form on demand. All you have to do is close your eyes and say, "In the name of the Evolver and Bestower of Forms," then you will transform immediately. However, you're still obligated to spend three days a month with dolphins. You can join any pod you choose; any pod will welcome you since you've become a wise dolphin. You must convey human wisdom to them and spread dolphins' morals among humans. That's the only way humans can pay attention to any other creature's wellbeing, other than their own, of course. That's how humans will fight to fix what some of their species' greed has destroyed. You will live in Tahiti, where you'll find papers, a house, and a whole life story that another previous human-dolphin prepared for you. You will know how to get there after your last jump from the mountain." "What about Arwa?" She answered me, "You'll find out yourself. Go send her in."

ARWA

I walked behind Ziad and the formerly old lady, who had now become young and beautiful. When they reached a cave that was hidden behind some thick, large trees, they entered as I waited for them outside. I tried to eavesdrop on them, but I couldn't hear a word. I began to ask myself, "What will I do when all of this is over?" I loved Ziad and I experienced feelings with him that I had never felt in my entire life. My soul was humbled by this experience, as it taught me how life came in many shapes and forms other than the ones I've known. I used to look at life through a needle's hole, but after that short experience, I was given a window as large as a mansion to contemplate life from and see it from different angles.

When Ziad returned, he asked me to enter the cave as "they" were waiting for me inside it. I didn't get who he was referring to: Could there be more than one woman inside? How many were there? Were they all young and attractive like the one I'd just met? The interior of the cave looked like a grand reception of a fancy house, with a pistachio-colored couch and a large chair that I was expected to sit on. Three ladies were sitting on the couch:

the one sitting in the middle was the woman I'd met earlier, while the two others sat on either side of her.

The woman in the middle spoke, "You must be asking yourself hundreds of questions. Go ahead and ask!" I tried to think, but all the questions suddenly evaporated from my head, so I asked, "How did you suddenly get so young and pretty?" The three ladies chuckled, then the one in the middle said, "We represent the spirit of the island. A spirit gets revived when it encounters a special dolphin, like Ziad, and a special beloved like you." I asked her, "Beloved?" to which she said, "That's the word we use when we speak about a woman that helps a dolphin win the privilege of full transformation."

I asked, "Can he have children? Normal children—" I began to ask, but I couldn't find the right phrasing for what I wanted to say. The three smiled and the one in the middle said, "Yes, he can. Normal children. For your information, he is extremely fertile, so he can father an entire tribe. Speaking of which, there is an actual tribe that lives in Fiji that belongs to that same species." I felt confused, so the woman asked, "Are you thinking about being with him for the rest of your life?" Defensively, I responded, "Are you two always this quiet?" so the one in the middle said, "I'm the only one who speaks here. So, what's your answer?"

I softly said, "Yes." The woman instantly let out an ululation and laughed, so I said aggressively, "What are you doing?" "Your lifelong commitment, dear, makes me very happy because true love is rare. What you two achieved hasn't happened in nearly half a century." I smiled despite myself, startled by her words. I was thinking about the same thing she was talking about as I analyzed how rare the love that smoothly evolved between us was, but I still had my questions. Every woman who develops feelings for a man initially thinks it's rare and unmatched. I even thought the same thing about my love for Kamel, but it turned out to be an empty delusion. The woman said, "Dolphins don't betray and they don't let you down either. Even though Ziad has become a real human, he was born a dolphin. That will always be a part of his identity." Angry at her for spying on my thoughts, I said, "Are you reading my mind?" The two women sitting on her sides shook their heads, but she didn't respond.

"There's a gift the island would like to offer you since you proved a rare nobility and kindness. You too will own the ability to transform into a dolphin whenever you choose. You can live your life normally, but if you're around the ocean and you want to transform, all you have to do is close your eyes and say, "In the name of the Evolver and Bestower of Forms." I swallowed nervously in disbelief as my heartbeat raced. I asked, "What if I wanted to go back to my normal life? Do I close my eyes and whistle like dolphins?" She said, "No, child. You will say the same prayer but in the dolphins' language. It seems like your intelligence level might stand in the way because dolphins are smarter than humans, and you have to become an intelligent human so you can transform whenever you want."

She was speaking sarcastically, but the excessive joy I felt at that moment had surpassed anything else. I had just learned I could try a new form of life whenever I wanted, then return to my normal lifestyle whenever I pleased. In addition to that, I was allowed to be with Ziad for the rest of my life. I didn't dare dream of anything greater. Even if I tried being a dolphin but didn't enjoy it, I could simply set that superpower aside and never transform again. Simple. She interrupted my thoughts and said, "But there's one rule." My heart sank in my chest, so she laughed and said, "Don't worry. It's a simple one. You have to climb to the top of the mountain with Ziad and jump in the water together. Just close your eyes and say, "In the name of the Evolver and Bestower of Forms" right before your body touches the water. Go ahead now, go."

I didn't want to discuss anything further, so I twirled around and attempted to leave the cave, thrilled to share the news with Ziad. Before I could leave, the woman said, "I forgot to tell you: if you happen to get pregnant, you won't be able to transform during those months." My face blushed, but I didn't respond. Instead, I got out of the cave and ran as fast as I could. Ziad awaited me outside, so I hugged him and gave him a long kiss. He was shocked at my unexplained happiness, so I grabbed his hand and informed him that I had officially become his, and he became mine. I pushed him in the direction of the mountain so we could climb it together, but when he asked for the reason I only said, "We're jumping together!" I couldn't share the news about me being able to transform with him yet, as I couldn't wrap my head around it even though it wasn't the strangest thing I learned in that place. We were able to climb the mountain together after some tripping and stumbling. Despite the difficulty of the process, I refused to stop, as if I had gained some sort of supernatural energy after learning my new fate. Ziad kept speaking about our future together enthusiastically, "I will have a name, a house, and an actual life, can you imagine? I will visit Egypt with you and we can get married there, then get back to Tahiti and live there." "Wait, there's something more important that has to happen first." "What is it?" I laughed and said, "We have to get back to Bora Bora. We'll jump from the mountain so the ocean can swallow us and return us to Bora Bora."

He was almost dancing with joy when he heard my words. I climbed the mountain with Ziad while contemplating every bit of him as if he was the most delightful and fulfilling fruit created by God. I felt elated as I climbed to the peak of the mountain and the peak of my golden years as well, without a single worry about the future. When we finally reached the top, which overlooked a breathtaking view, I didn't feel scared despite how steep it looked. I simply held Ziad's hand, brought it to my lips, and kissed it. He then took mine and did the same thing, as we both stood on the edge. He spoke loudly, "Jump as high as you can." I nodded understandingly. We took three steps backward then we started running together, finally making our grand jump as we held each other's hands.

Just like we previously swam, ate, laughed, and went through different phases of love together, we were now flying together. We were tickled by the air that seemed to be celebrating the two of us. The waves and rocks beneath us looked like they were taking part in a large orchestra ensemble, in honor of our entrance. Even the fish were jumping in joy, thrilled for our arrival. As our bodies approached the water, I closed my eye and whispered, "In the name of the Evolver and Bestower of forms," then I heard a startled gasp from Ziad before our bodies touched the ocean.

The size of my body effortlessly extended as we dove deep in the water, without feeling any kind of pain or discomfort. We had both transformed into dolphins at the same moment, as the water continued to make smooth waves around us. I jumped in the air as our bodies danced together before we dove again into the water. I whistled lovingly, "I love you."

THE END

www.ingramcontent.com/pod-product-compliance
Lightning Source LLC
LaVergne TN
LVHW091300150826
845673LV00006B/1487